MANAGERIALLY SPEAKING

MANAGERIALLY SPEAKING

A Common Sense Approach
To Business Leadership

A proven approach to empower staff
and create cohesive organizations

Marcel Gingras

Library and Archives Canada Cataloguing in Publication

Gingras, Marcel, 1952-
      Managerially speaking: a common sense approach to business leadership / Marcel Gingras; Janet Dimond, editor.

Includes bibliographical references.
ISBN 0-9737577-0-1

      1. Business   2. Management.   3. Leadership.
I. Dimond, Janet   II. Title.

HD57.7.G528 2005   658.4'092   C2005-901172-6

PRINTED IN CANADA

To Jocelyne, my wife,
and to my children Marc-Olivier, Liliane and Vincent

Special Thanks
and Acknowledgements

I want to thank all those who have made this book possible. Special thanks to Patty Edwards, who assisted me to manage the publication of this book while I was busy working on other projects. Without her, this book would never have been published. I also want to acknowledge the work of Janet Dimond, who did a wonderful job editing this book while preserving my preference for communication style.

I also want to acknowledge the contribution of a number of people who submitted their comments during a period of several months while I was distributing some of the chapters in the form of a monthly newsletter. I'm also grateful to a number of people who submitted ideas for additional topics, and to those who submitted ideas for the final title of the book, including my great friend Mario Galizia, whose suggestion for a title was the one that was retained.

I also wish to convey my appreciation to Don Stewart, CEO of Sun Life Financial at the time of writing this book, to have put his confidence in me early in my career. Don hired me for a middle management position, which was quite a stretch at that stage of my career, and I'm thankful for his confidence and his mentorship during those years.

Finally, I want to thank Cathy Honor who, several years ago, planted the seed in my mind about publishing a book related to leadership and management. I had never imagined that I would ever publish a book and without Cathy's encouragement, I'm quite certain that this project would never have started.

Contents

Introduction

I can hardly believe I'm about to put the finishing touches on a book. I have to pinch myself to realize this isn't a dream – this is reality. I never intended to write a book. For close to 30 years I climbed the corporate ladder to the point where I had an organization of close to 5,000 people reporting to me. Then, through a corporate merger, my job disappeared and I ended up accepting another corporate job which didn't bring me the expected challenge and satisfaction. At that point, I decided to give up my corporate job and start my own general management consulting business.

Initially, I needed to meet people to introduce my services. However, I also needed to keep my name in front of existing and potential clients. I came up with the idea of writing monthly newsletters covering different topics related to the leadership and management skills required in running organizations. As it turned out, I ended up covering over 20 different topics. As newsletters continued to accumulate, several of my contacts encouraged me to use the existing material and turn it into a book. Obviously I needed some work to reorganize the content, but essentially this book was written over a period of close to two years.

It's hard to believe this project is nearing completion. I'm not a writer, a trained management consultant, nor an academic. Typically, management books have come from these sources. By training, I'm an actuary. Traditionally actuaries have written technical books, not management books. However I'm not a traditional actuary. I have done some actuarial work but for most of my career, I've occupied management roles.

When I took my first management job, I was made responsible for a group of 40 people in a field where I had little expertise. I didn't have much management training except for some leadership training I received during the nine years I spent in the Armed Forces. Five of those years were at a military college where the emphasis was clearly on completion of an academic degree. Even during my active career in the Armed Forces, I never really had people reporting to me. Following that, I occupied a couple of technical jobs until I was given the opportunity to take on this first management job, responsible for this group of 40 people.

To this day, I still wonder why I was given this job. It was either because my employer saw some potential in me or was desperate to put someone into the job. In any event, I was ill-prepared technically and from a management standpoint to take it. In hindsight, being ill-prepared technically was probably a blessing in disguise, as it forced me to focus on the managerial aspect of the job, and come up with ways to understand the business without learning every technical detail. It also forced me to perform the job at a higher level than if I'd been more knowledgeable technically.

Given my lack of knowledge and training in leadership and management, how did I learn? The sad truth is I learned like most other people – on the fly. I was fortunate to have a good mentor when I took my first management job. Over the years, I attended some training sessions and seminars on the topic of management. I did some reading. I also learned from some of my own employees, many of whom ended up having very successful careers. However, the important point is that I had to learn by myself. In several respects, I had to go with my instincts. I had a few good role models, but not that many. I saw plenty of bad ones from whom I learned how *not* to do things. I don't remember seeing any form of comprehensive framework to teach me how to lead and manage. I saw bits and pieces but not something I could readily apply. I'm sure it must exist in some form, but I never had ready access to it.

A lot has been written in the area of leadership and management. A lot of the material has been produced by academics and management consultants. However, much of it lacks the strong connection required to put these concepts into practice. Many executives have tremendous experience in how to lead and manage, but lack the time and appetite to sit back and document their approach to running their business.

Since I gave up my corporate job, I've had the opportunity to reflect on various approaches I've observed over my career, and to figure out a way to express my approach in a cohesive way. I've also had the luxury of having the time to put it into writing. This book is my contribution to this fascinating topic. I don't have the academic or literary credentials of others who have written on this topic. What I *do* have is a lot of practical experience and a good intuitive feeling to determine what might work and what might not.

As you'll see in Chapter 2, running an organization is like operating a machine. The machine has a given amount of potential. Most organizations are like machines. They have the potential to deliver some output. However, much of that potential is wasted for several reasons which are described in Chapter 2 and explored in further detail in the remaining chapters. Much of the potential is wasted due to the leader's inability to lead, and the manager's inability to manage. In several organizations, the desire to produce quick, spectacular results is overtaking the need to develop a solid foundation required to build a sustainable, performing organization.

This book isn't intended to revolutionize the art of leadership and management. Rather, it's my humble contribution to the practical aspect of this topic, based on thirty years of experience. I want to thank you for taking the time to read this book. I hope that reading it fulfills your expectations and that you'll gain value from it.

In management thirty years' experience does not count for much if it merely means ten times three of the same experience.
    – Neil J. McKinnon, Banker

Chapter I

So What Have I Learned?

During the time I spent in management, I learned that managing and leading people can be fun and in the end, it should be pretty simple. Unfortunately, a lot of people have tried to turn management and leadership into what it was never really meant to be: the application of complex principles which appear to be recreated with passing generations of management gurus. Management principles should be simple and withstand the passage of time.

Here we'll discuss four basic principles I've developed over the years.

High deltas are bad news

I've always been amazed that some people seem to behave very differently depending on circumstances and the people they're dealing with. I've observed several people who appeared to be so nice and accommodating to me as their leader, and yet I would hear they were miserable to deal with from the point of view of their staff or peers. Then I started to refer to such people as having a *high differential* or *high delta factor.*

For example, estimate on a scale of 1 to 10 (10 being the nicest someone can be) how nice John, one of your managers, appears to be when dealing with you as his boss. Let's call this the *b* factor. Then, measure on the same scale how nice John is when dealing with his staff, and call this the *s* factor. Therefore the delta factor is simply *b* minus *s*, and the result can be either positive or negative.

- Let's assume that John is very nice to his boss and has a b factor of 9, and isn't so nice to his staff and has an s factor of 3. Therefore, John's delta factor would be equal to 6.
- Likewise, Mary is very difficult to deal with from her boss' perspective and has a b factor of 4; however, she is very easygoing with her employees and has an s factor of 8. Therefore Mary's delta factor is -4.

So, as a manager, would you prefer to have John or Mary as one of your direct reports? I wouldn't really want either one of them. It's likely that John is *acting* when he's dealing with me and is telling me what I want to hear. He may even praise me excessively to feed my ego. John is likely to be a dictator when dealing with his staff and would expect total obedience from them. Obviously this is a pretty bad mix.

What about Mary? Well, Mary may be one of those people managing using a *bunker* mentality. She'll fight tooth and nail for her employees, trying to resist changes that may be suggested by her boss, and will likely be very popular with her own employees. Mary will probably go back to her staff and tell them how *they* (senior management) are trying to impose changes on her, and how she's fighting for her employees.

So, make no mistake, high deltas, whether positive or negative, aren't good for any organization. More than likely, you have some in your own organization. The tricky part is to find them!

Rule of three

As I moved up the corporate ladder, I found it more and more difficult to make an accurate assessment of people or situations, simply because of lack of exposure. Some of my direct reports were in a different location and typically would at least be on a different floor. It was even worse when it came to forming an opinion on people who didn't report directly to me, just because of the lack of exposure. Then the question of how much information is needed to form an opinion becomes critical. Forming quick judgements based on one incident is typically unfair, as I might not understand everything around the issue that came to my attention. Waiting forever to form an opinion and take action is called *procrastination*. Then my compromise became the so-called *rule of three*.

In its simplest form, the rule of three works as follows. The first time I heard something negative about somebody, I just made a mental note. I would try to disregard the information on the basis that the information provided to me might have been incomplete. The second time I heard something similar, I would really get interested, as I felt there was probably a 90% chance the information might be accurate. The third time, this became my new reality and I would take action or push for appropriate action.

This may sound somewhat drastic. However, the point is that as a senior person you can't be so quick to assess that you're unfair to people, and you can't be so slow that you feel you never have enough information to form an appropriate judgement.

Rewiring your staff

I've always been amazed that managers feel they can engineer major personality changes in the people reporting to them. My experience is that such changes are highly unlikely to happen, and if they do, they only happen for short periods of time. Every one of us is wired a certain way, due to genes, culture, family environment, and life experience in general. So how much time should you spend rewiring your staff?

I'm a strong believer in training, especially in the early stages of people's careers. Training creates awareness and allows people to discover more quickly what might otherwise take years to learn. However, there's a huge difference between training people to do things a certain way, and expecting them to have major changes in personality.

As an example, I've sat through several succession planning sessions. This is typically the best forum in which to observe people dreaming in colour regarding what employees need to do to become better managers. Sometimes people would mention that Tom could be a great manager except for the fact that he was a very poor communicator. Then someone would suggest that Tom should go on a communication course. Sometimes I would ask, "How old is Tom and how long has he been managing?" People would sometimes push back and ask why my question was relevant. Well, Tom might have been 50 years old and might have been a manager for 15 years. Essentially, my view was that at 50, Tom wasn't likely to be rewired, and after 15 years as a manager, he should pretty well have figured out how to communicate, assuming he had the proper attributes to be a good manager. Had Tom been 31 with 1 year of managerial experience, I would've been much more receptive to give training or coaching a fighting chance to create some major improvement.

People come with their strengths and weaknesses. You don't have to accept all their weaknesses. You still have to try to cause incremental improvement in your staff, or make a personnel change if their weaknesses are more than you can tolerate. However, I've always had greater success leveraging people's strengths rather than trying to expect their weaknesses to disappear.

So, how much rewiring do you really think you can do? How much do you really believe you can do in yourself? Don't expect too much more from others!

Marriage doesn't (generally) improve your future partner

Before we get into a debate on this topic, read on!

Let's talk about recruiting. I must admit I've seen a lot of poor recruiting in my career, including some I've done myself. Generally, disappointing recruiting is the result of one of several factors including poor interview techniques, improper reference checks, the lack of care to help the newcomer fit within the organization, and last but not least, the belief that the person will change somewhat once on board.

Imagine this scenario: Your VP Finance and CFO resigned in July. You started a search immediately with the expectation that you should have someone available within a couple of months. It's summertime and difficult to schedule meetings, so now you're into late October and year-end is fast approaching! You finally have a shortlist of three but the first candidate is much stronger than the other two. Number two might do the job, but you're not sure and aren't keen on number three. You make an offer to number one who decides not to accept it. So now you decide you should go with number two, Jane. You do more in-depth reference checks and find out Jane has a history of being difficult to manage because she has a knack for upsetting people around her. Sound familiar? So, what do you do? Well, now it's mid-November and year-end is really getting close.

So what's the compromise? Oftentimes you'll hire Jane, but will really coach her to be more accommodating so that she'll stop upsetting people in the future. You probably know it won't happen, but after a while you convince yourself it really will. Jane comes on board and soon she upsets a whole bunch of people – your life is miserable. So are you really surprised? Don't expect marriage to substantially improve your future partner!

The sheep are without the shepherds: they are disoriented,
bewildered, lost. Indeed what is true of the sheep, can also be true
of the shepherds as well: they too can be disoriented, bewildered, lost.
  – Bernard J.F. Lonergan, Jesuit Philosopher

Chapter 2

Why is the Machine Leaking?

Over the course of my career, I've had the opportunity to work with organizations of various sizes. I've worked with an organization employing close to 100,000 people, a couple with 10,000 people, and a couple with less than 500 people. Up until recently, I had never tried to work with an organization of just one – me working on my own.

This has given me the opportunity to see more clearly the advantages and disadvantages of working with both very small and very large organizations. At one end of the spectrum, I now have to do everything: sales, marketing, administration, and delivery of work. I can't afford a number of tools and the specialization that many large organizations take for granted, and as a result, I'm not as efficient as I could otherwise be.

On the other hand, I know exactly what I want to do and how I want to do it. I don't waste time in internal meetings. I'm very focused and proud of what I'm doing. So I'm quite efficient on that front.

On balance, I assume that proportionally speaking, mid-size and large organizations should be at least as efficient as me, or any other owner-operated business – possibly quite a bit more given their access to capital, technology, and savings created through economies of scale. Most organizations are far from being proportionally as efficient as they should be, and therefore fail to realize their full potential, or if you prefer, they're leaking to varying degrees.

What's the issue?

Essentially, I believe that an organization with 1,000 employees, for example, should be at least 1,000 times more productive than an organization with 1 employee. I don't have any data to suggest this is true; however, my experience is that for most organizations, the number is likely to be somewhat below or well below 1,000. In any event, it's pretty certain the number is well below where it should be, given the well-publicized synergies and economies of scale.

These economies of scale and gains attributable to specialization by function are often negated by the added complexity and resulting confusion in the organization. Obviously, this isn't universally true of every organization; however, it is true that every organization has room for improvement.

Why do most organizations fail to realize their full potential?

There are a variety of reasons why organizations are leaking. Here are some of the major sources and root causes of leakage existing in varying degrees in most organizations of any size:

- **Unclear vision**. In many organizations, many people don't understand the vision of the enterprise. They don't understand it because it doesn't exist – it hasn't been communicated or it's not being reinforced continuously to existing and new employees.
- **Communication**. In many organizations, communication isn't as well organized as it could be. Even if it is, the time required for leaders to communicate and for employees to capture the information becomes a source of reduced productivity. Keep in mind that my starting point is an enterprise with a sole employee, where no time is allocated to internal communication.
- **Pride**. One of the main drivers for sole operators is the pride they have for the work they do. If they wish to stay in business, they have no choice but to be proud. In larger organizations, it's a mammoth task to create pride. It can be done; however, it's difficult. Over the years, I've always been amazed at the amount of internal criticism directed at organizations, quite often by senior and/or long-term employees. Hardly a recipe for success!
- **Focus**. Again, smaller enterprises need to focus on what really matters – otherwise the enterprise is unlikely to stay alive for very long. In larger organizations, there's quite a bit of leakage because people sometimes focus on things that don't really matter or activities with low added value, or even worse, negative added value. As an example, I recently tried to subscribe to a magazine and had been warned that my application would take six weeks to process. What has gone wrong for an organization to take six weeks to accept my simple, straightforward business?

- **Politics**. Not surprisingly, as soon as you bring more than one person into a company, there will be politics. Hopefully, there won't be much but it'll still be there. People will always have some kind of personal agenda. Some organizations are known to be real political nests, and as a result there's major leakage in productivity.
- **Teamwork**. Teams of one are quite team focused by definition. In fact, it hardly qualifies as a team. Ideally, teams of more than one should enjoy the same unity in perspective and execution as a team of one. Some teams work very well together; however, it typically doesn't happen by accident. It requires a fair amount of time investment. However, many teams lack the ideal uniformity and the result is even worse – lack of uniformity in direction and execution.
- **Mindset**. With small organizations, it's easier to have a uniform mindset or culture (the set of values and principles accepted within the organization). In larger organizations, there may be different mindsets or subcultures. Merger and acquisition activity generally compound the challenge.
- **Leadership and management**. In very small organizations, leadership isn't so critical, especially if there are no employees other than the owner. However, in large organizations leadership and management competencies are critical, yet many organizations suffer from a lack of these skills. A number of people who are in leadership roles behave as if their role were managerial (they manage things as opposed to leading people). In most enterprises, the leakage attributable to this shortcoming is huge.

- **Organizational design**. As companies grow, they need to spend more time on organizational design. Some suffer from poor design and others are known to change the design continuously, resulting in confusion and wasted time.

- **Empowerment**. In small companies, people need to be resourceful to survive and there tend to be few barriers to getting things done. In larger organizations, convincing people that they're empowered to do things is a major challenge. In other organizations, people are really not empowered to do much without a lot of bureaucratic involvement. Both of these situations lead to wasted time as people wait for somebody else to do something.

- **Sense of ownership**. The beauty of operating a small business is that there's direct linkage between action and results. In most organizations, it's difficult to create that sense of ownership beyond a limited number of people at the top of the organization. As a result, people behave as if they're handling someone else's business as opposed to their own. Many organizations do a good job of trying to create that sense of ownership; however, many don't.

- **Creativity**. Due to the heavy bureaucracy afflicting many organizations, it's difficult for people to convey ideas, get them accepted, and implement them. After a while, this kills creativity within the organization. It's difficult to create a climate conducive to creativity. It's much easier to create a climate where it doesn't exist.

- **Meetings**. In most organizations, there's a huge amount of time spent in meetings. Yet many organizations allow a vast amount of resources to be wasted because there are too many meetings that last too long, are attended by too many people, and quite often without specific or measurable outcome. Companies have all types of controls on hard-cost spending, yet they sometimes allow anyone to call a meeting that may cost $2,000 once the full cost is recognized.

- **Financial focus**. Small enterprises quickly understand the basics of finance. Revenues must exceed expenses by some margin and positive cash flow is most desirable. This financial focus gets lost as organizations grow. Eventually, except for a few people, employees tend not to see the whole financial picture, and eventually assume that managing the financial aspect isn't part of their job.

What can be done?

One of the responsibilities of leaders is to create and communicate a vision for the enterprise. They must also create an environment that is conducive to handling business as effectively as possible. As part of creating the right environment, leaders must pay attention to the sources of leakage within the organization (areas where the organization is failing to realize its full potential). Each potential source of leakage needs to be reviewed systematically and continuously.

In future chapters, we'll look at most of the areas mentioned in the previous section, along with some examples of how incremental improvement can be made in each.

Summary

Based on experience working directly and indirectly with several organizations, every company has several sources of leakage. The issue isn't whether your own machine is leaking, but to determine how much leakage exists, and how long you can afford to wait before you fix it.

In any great organization it is far, far safer to be wrong with the majority than to be right alone.
    – John Kenneth Galbraith, U.S. Economist

Chapter 3

Organizational Mindset – Do You Have One? Do You Need One?

In the previous chapter, we identified several reasons why most organizations fail to perform at their full potential. There were over a dozen factors described as leakage sources within organizations. In the next chapters, we'll discuss most of these factors in greater detail. One of these elements of leakage is the absence of a cohesive organizational mindset. It's not a coincidence that this is the first leakage source I chose to examine in this book. I selected it because it's complex, difficult to explain in a manner that is understandable, and is an area where I feel many organizations don't do a very good job, resulting in wasted energy within corporate structures.

Mindset defined

The dictionary defines *mindset* as *ideas and attitudes with which a person approaches a situation, especially when these are seen as difficult to alter.* By extension, an *organizational mindset* can be defined as *ideas and attitudes with which an organization*

Chapter 3—Organizational Mindset – Do You Have One? Do You Need One?

16

approaches situations. It's often described as *organizational culture.* However, *culture* is an overused word in the corporate environment, and people are often uncertain as to what it really means. So my preference has always been to refer to this as *organizational mindset* or *shared mindset.*

An organizational mindset represents a very complex mix resulting from several factors:

- organizations are made up of a large number of individuals, each with different backgrounds
- companies may be in multiple geographical locations
- people may have come from different companies due to past merger activity
- ongoing movement in management and the employee population in general.

There are several elements which help shape and define the mindset of an organization:

- vision as expressed by management and whether it has credibility within the organization
- types of people in the organization, how they interact and operate
- decision-making process
- preference for consensus building versus dictating directions
- support for entrepreneurship
- idea generation process (bottom up or top down)
- sense of empowerment versus organizational paralysis

- communication process
- information sharing
- reward system (team versus individual)
- objective setting process
- management systems
- project management discipline or lack of
- expected collaboration among businesses and between business units and support units
- attitude toward customer service
- approach toward employees
- trust level between management and employees and among employees themselves
- problem resolution preference (how an organization likes to deal with problems and issues)
- accountability setting and discipline in holding people accountable.

Why does it matter?

Creating a shared mindset within an organization can make a huge difference between a great organization and a mediocre one. It's difficult to believe that an organization can enjoy sustainable success without having a solid organizational mindset that can survive the passage of time (not one that changes regularly depending on the mood of its leaders).

An organizational mindset brings about these benefits:

- For senior management, it helps create peace of mind, as they can gain some level of assurance decisions made in

Chapter 3—Organizational Mindset – Do You Have One? Do You Need One?

18

the organization follow a pattern, with which they would be as comfortable as if they were part of every single decision being made within the organization.

- It helps to promote consistency in execution.
- It provides external stakeholders with a feeling of cohesiveness in approach as they deal with different individuals and different parts of the organization.
- It reduces waste within the organization as it contributes to eliminating the potential for conflicts.

What does it take to create a sustainable organizational mindset?

Establishing a shared mindset within the organization is one of the most critical leadership functions; however, it's often a function that's neglected because it's complex, multifaceted, and takes time for results to show up. Sometimes people resort to quick fixes to get results, not recognizing that time invested in creating a shared mindset is highly leveraged, and is the most effective way to create a lasting, successful organization.

The accountability for creating an organizational mindset belongs to people at the top of the organization, whether it's a company, division or department. Ideally the mindset creation should start at the highest possible level within the organization. However, it's still possible for intermediate managers to work on this, even though the mindset may not be clearly established at higher levels.

There are several actions that leaders can and must take to create an environment with a distinctive mindset:

- Create a compelling vision for the organization.
- Communicate the vision directly in a manner understandable by the majority of employees. Written vision and mission statements may help; however, they seldom do the job unless reinforced using many different tools and forums.
- Recruit people who fit within the ideal mindset. Talented people with the wrong values and/or wrong attitudes may send a strong signal that management isn't serious about the environment it wants to create.
- Eliminate people who can't operate within the ideal environment. People get their cues from what leaders do, not what they say.
- Create a management team who believes in what they're doing and who are passionate about it. Passion is contagious – so is lack of passion.
- Favour team players as opposed to pure technical talent. Obviously a healthy mix of both is desirable.
- Encourage people to follow a disciplined logical approach to dealing with issues, so decisions may be replicated over time.
- Develop role models who exemplify the ideal organizational values. People can learn quickly from role models and it's a very effective way to spread the ideal mindset throughout the organization. It's much easier to spread the message if there are many bearers of the same message.

Chapter 3—Organizational Mindset – Do You Have One? Do You Need One?

20

- Have leaders actively involved in their organization, so people can see them in action and learn from them.
- Encourage consistency in decision making, so people know what to expect from their management group.
- Preach by example. Nice speeches not supported by action give rise to disbelief and sarcasm within the employee group.
- Use every opportunity to share the knowledge base. It's easier for people to reach similar conclusions if they have access to the same information.
- Communicate often, to different groups and in a consistent manner. People shouldn't have to guess what their leaders have in mind.
- Discourage politics within the organization.
- Create an organizational model. I've reproduced an organizational model here that we've used in the past. Essentially it's represented by a set of wheels or gears, all of which are moving at the same time. The message is that every moving piece has an impact somewhere else in the organization, and people have to be conscious of this fact. The model also shows how decisions are made at certain levels and implemented everywhere in the organization. Obviously this is one of many models that can be used; however, it helped people figure out how we wanted to operate as an organization. Which model you use doesn't really matter, as long as you have a model understood by people in the organization.

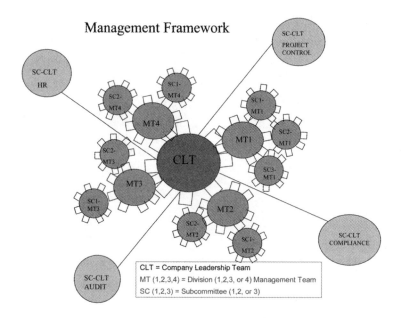

Management Framework

CLT = Company Leadership Team
MT (1,2,3,4) = Division (1,2,3, or 4) Management Team
SC (1,2,3) = Subcommittee (1,2, or 3)

Summary

A shared organizational mindset is key in creating a highly effective organization. However, it's important to keep in mind that it doesn't get created by accident. It can't be mandated. It demands hard work and confidence that all the right elements are in place. It requires a major time investment on the part of leaders at various organizational levels. It also takes time for results to show up and therefore patience is needed. However, if all the right elements are in place, mindset convergence will eventually happen – and then the organization will enjoy high rewards for its efforts.

Management is maintaining the status quo; leadership is setting a new direction.
    – George Torok, Motivational Speaker

Chapter 4

Leadership and Management

In Chapter 2, we identified several reasons why many organizations fail to perform at their full potential. We reviewed the absence of a cohesive mindset as a great source of leakage or underperformance within many organizations. In this chapter, we'll analyze a second major source of leakage, represented by a lack of focus in developing and nurturing leadership and management skills. There are organizations that do a great job at developing good leaders and managers; however, there are many who only pay lip service to these critical elements required to run an efficient organization.

Leadership and management – is it all one and the same?

There's generally quite a bit of confusion between the two words. A lot of people use them interchangeably. Yet there's a sea of difference between the two. The dictionary defines *leadership* as *the ability to lead* (which in turn is defined as *the ability to inspire, induce and influence*). *Management* is defined as *the ability to administer and use resources such as time and materials in a skillful way.*

Some people are great managers but poor leaders. Some great leaders lack management skills but can still be successful if they're able to surround themselves with great managers. Management can be complex but can also be somewhat mechanical in nature, despite the fact that good managers generally use a good dose of intuition. Leadership comes from the heart, and ranks high on the intuitive scale as it requires ongoing adjustments to changing circumstances and personalities.

Why do some organizations suffer from poor leadership?

There are many organizations who suffer from poor leadership at various levels. This results from the fact that many organizations recruit mostly for technical competencies and hope that leaders will eventually emerge. It's possible to train managers with some success, although some people may never be able to manage effectively. It's much more difficult to train people to become leaders. Many people believe leaders are born that way, and given the right environment, will thrive in leadership roles because they have the right stuff for it. Training can provide incremental leadership ability; however, training tends to work better with people who already have the basic abilities.

Leadership requires good intuition. What comes to mind as an example is a memory of Sasha, our 16-pound Jack Russell terrier, on the day she decided to attack a large German shepherd. The German shepherd was walking with his owner on the sidewalk in front of our house. I believe it had behaved inappropriately (from Sasha's standpoint) a few months earlier and Sasha saw her opportunity to seek revenge. She jumped at the dog's throat, which was the right thing to do if you accept she had her reasons to attack. Without any training, she knew intuitively what to do. The fact that she exercised poor judgement in the first place, and would've been dead meat had it not been for the presence of the German shepherd's owner, is beside the point.

A sad example of poor intuitive feeling is a real-life story that was related to me. An employee had gone to see his manager early in the morning and insisted on seeing him right away. His manager was very focused on preparing for an upcoming meeting, didn't recognize on the spot the need to pay immediate attention, and suggested instead they meet later in the day. A couple of hours later, the employee made his way to the roof of the building and jumped to his death.

I've had the opportunity to spend a few years in the Armed Forces. Essentially, they were recruiting officer cadets based on perceived leadership skills and ability to learn. Their view was that the technical specialty wasn't that important at that stage. Leadership *potential* is what they were looking for. I doubt that many organizations recruit for leadership potential unless they're recruiting at senior levels. Most organizations recruit for specialists, and train them to become better specialists until there's a need to promote someone to a managerial role. Even then, some organizations provide no or limited training to help people make the transition to their new role. Not surprisingly, many managers and people in leadership roles see themselves as superspecialists (managing more of what they've been trained to do, as opposed to making the transition to becoming general managers).

This situation is most noticeable in professional companies such as accounting, consulting, and legal firms, etc., where succession planning is generally a major issue, as it's not uncommon for the firm to have limited talent to lead and manage it.

Where to start?

A few years ago, we recruited someone in an organizational development role. The person had been recruited by someone else, but when she came on board, I had to explain to her what my expectations were for this newly created role. I told her that, in my opinion, out of our few hundred people in management and leadership roles, only 80% or so should be in these roles. Out of those who were suitable, I told her my assumption was that they operated at 80% capacity due to lack of training or proper role models from whom they could learn. So I told her that essentially the organization was operating at 64% (0.8 x 0.8) effectiveness in what I considered to be extremely critical roles in the organization. Whether we were at 50%, 64% or 75% wasn't that important. The issue was that we were well below where I thought we should be.

From that point on, we started putting the focus on trying to work on competencies required for people to be considered for hire or promotion to the management levels. We also worked at repositioning those who had made it to the management ranks, despite their lack of skills. And finally, we started working at closing the gap between actual and required skills for those who had the potential to become good managers, but had not been provided the right opportunity to learn what could be learned through formal training.

Finally, there's no better way than to learn from people who are good leaders and managers (having people who are good role models). If your organization isn't solid at the top levels from a leadership and managerial standpoint, people at lower levels won't have the opportunity to learn from role models. In fact, they may get confused by the mixed signals they're getting from leaders and managers with inadequate skills. So, external recruiting may become necessary to accelerate the process.

A few areas where managers and leaders should focus

I've had the opportunity to review employee survey results administered on a pretty large scale. I've always been fascinated by the differences observed among groups performing similar functions. Sometimes the only noticeable difference was the manager of the group. Yet satisfaction gaps might have been huge despite the fact that the nature of the work and compensation would've been the same. The only conclusion I could reach was that the approach taken by managers made a huge difference in how employees felt about the workplace.

Generally, good leaders distinguish themselves by following many or all of these principles:

- They listen and pay attention to people around them.
- They see their role as that of an integrator/coordinator as opposed to being a superspecialist.

- They look for changing trends. They're quick to notice changing trends and behaviour and accordingly, can address issues much more quickly.
- They're good at replacing uncertainty by certainty (they make their position and expectations clear, and don't leave it to employees to guess where they stand).
- They're good at providing feedback, whether positive or negative. They recognize that people like to know where they stand.
- They provide direction to the organization and in doing so, contribute to enhancing the collective mindset of the organization.
- They share information widely, as required and possible, to enlarge collective knowledge.
- They create a fun environment in which people can get serious when it's time to be serious, and can relax together when it's appropriate to do so.
- They follow up religiously on their commitments.
- They preach by example. I've witnessed senior people preaching the sense of urgency and would then sit on minor decisions and straightforward paperwork for weeks, destroying any credibility they might have had.

This list wasn't meant to be exhaustive; however, it's certainly a good starting point where people can focus their efforts on making a major difference in how they discharge their responsibilities as managers and leaders.

Summary

Based on experience dealing directly and indirectly with several organizations, many of these organizations have some leakage, or untapped potential, in the area of leadership and management. There's huge potential for those who choose to invest time and effort in this area. It's difficult to imagine any organization enjoying sustainable success without a solid management and leadership base. Rewards are there to be reaped for those who choose to pursue this opportunity.

People are very, very hungry for some kind of contact with
a greater world than one which they can immediately perceive.
  – Robertson Davies, Man-of-letters

Chapter 5

I Don't See the Vision

In this chapter, we'll investigate another source of leakage – the failure of many organizations to communicate a well-articulated vision to their employees.

A lot has been written in the area of mission and vision statements. We won't reinvent the wheel here; rather, the focus is on exploring ways to share the real vision (as opposed to the words describing it) with the rest of the organization, in a manner such that employees will understand it and be able to apply it in a manner consistent with the vision of its leaders. I believe the definition here is precise enough for the purpose of this chapter. You can observe several variations of what's intended by vision statements by reviewing those of several companies, generally available through the Internet.

What does *vision* really mean?

Vision is defined as *the ability of great perception, especially of future developments*. In the corporate arena, vision is generally understood to mean the view of the organizational leaders as to what the organization should be, how it wishes to conduct business, be perceived in the marketplace, and position itself compared to the rest of the marketplace.

Why is it important to have a vision and be able to communicate it?

It's quite obvious that organizations are highly unlikely to succeed unless they have a vision of where they want to go. Based on the old saying that it's difficult to get to your destination if you don't know where you're going, having a clear vision is a critical step to lead the organization. Although this is a necessary condition to success, it's not sufficient. Other stakeholders also need to understand what the vision is. Customers, shareholders, and board members all have a need to understand it. However, the most important group is the employees. If they don't understand it, they're unlikely to be able to operate in a manner that reflects the objectives of their leaders.

In smaller companies, it's important that the vision be shared with employees. In these small companies, it's somewhat easier to accomplish. However, in large diversified companies, it becomes critical to invest significant amounts of time to make sure the vision is shared with and understood by as many employees as possible.

In many organizations people are recruited, and limited efforts are made to share the vision with the newcomers who then struggle for months or years to figure out what their new company stands for. There was a time when I wasn't a great believer in spending too much time creating and communicating vision, mission and values. My view was that, as a family, my wife and I never had to spend time on these things and we ended up with children sharing similar values. However, someone correctly pointed out to me that the workplace is different. People join the organization at different stages in their lives, with different cultural backgrounds, work and life experiences. So it's unlikely that putting together a diversified group of people is going to result in a cohesive entity, unless every managerial level is willing to invest time to create the ideal state of cohesiveness. Therefore, there's a need to create and share a vision for the organization along with an accompanying mission statement and values.

Where to start?

There are several steps required before the vision can be understood broadly within the organization. First, let's state the obvious: a vision must exist before it can be shared. It may sound funny, but I've been associated directly or indirectly with some organizations that appeared to operate in spite of the fact that their leaders didn't seem to really have a clear vision.

Creating and *sharing* vision is a key component of leadership and is part of the very important role of creating a collective or shared mindset within the organization. Once created, the vision will transpire throughout, but only to the extent that its leaders support the vision through their actions, as this is where people generally take their cues.

Sometimes firms use consultants to go through the process of creating a vision and communicating it. Sometimes consultants can help put a disciplined process in place; however, the guts of the vision must come from the leaders of the organization.

These steps are required to create and communicate the vision for the organization:

1. The vision should be arrived at either independently by the CEO or in collaboration with the executive group. The focus should be on having a clear vision as opposed to the words used to express it. Some organizations spend little time discussing the real vision and a lot of time, sometimes months, arguing about the words. Expressing the vision in concise words is important, but only after the real vision has been created.

2. The next step should be to test the vision with a number of people in the organization. It's fairly common for employees not to understand what their leaders were thinking when they came out with the vision statement. It's important to make sure it makes sense to the average person and it must be realizable.

3. Once feedback has been received, the vision statement should be confirmed (is it going to accomplish what's intended and if not, changes should be made).

4. Last but not least is the implementation stage. The vision must be communicated to people within the organization, along with the associated mission statement and values. This step requires a lot of time and energy. Many organizations fail to help employees understand what its

leaders have in mind. They spend a lot of time creating statements and tag lines, but insufficient time communicating what's really expected, using a language that can reach the average person in the organization.

Where things generally go wrong

It's fairly common for organizations to have a real vision, yet they can't get the expected benefits from having created a vision and mission statement. There are several reasons why this may happen:

- Executives have difficulty understanding what the average person in their organization understands. I remember getting frustrated because several months into a change program, some people around me seemed to *not get it*. At some point, I came around to the fact that I might be the one not getting it. I hadn't spent enough time explaining the vision and why I felt it was the right one.
- On occasion, vision statements may be taken from too high a level. As an example, many organizations say they want to be a world-class provider. There's nothing inherently wrong with this, especially if this is what the company aspires to be. However, for the average person, this won't help them much as they have no context in which to understand what it takes to *be* a world-class provider.

- A lot of vision statements represent more of a wish list than guiding principles for the organization. The end result is that employees look at this sort of vision statement with scepticism, as it doesn't connect with what they observe on a daily basis.
- Sometimes vision statements which might otherwise work fail, because they end up being used for the wrong purpose. As an example, I heard of a consulting firm whose vision statement referred to being able to offer all of its diversified services to its clients. The statement was then posted in the main reception area. When clients looked at this, their reaction was that they were about to be invaded by a bunch of consultants from other practices trying to cross-sell additional services.
- I've seen vision statements refer to standards of client service which employees look at with scepticism, because the firm may not have invested in technology, training, or recruiting to allow the vision to be realizable.
- Lastly, for too many companies, their vision is to make money. There's nothing wrong with making money; in fact, it's rather nice. However, this is somewhat unhelpful to the average person who is too far away from the point where profits are accounted for. Vision has to go deeper than this. It has to address the fundamentals of how the firm will do business and generally, if the vision is right and well executed, profits will emerge.

Sustaining vision

Once a vision has been created and communicated, it's important to be able to sustain it within the organization. These actions should be taken to ensure the vision continues to be relevant and understood by most employees:

- It has to be communicated to new employees as they join the organization. It can become time consuming; however, it's worth the time being invested.
- It's critical that leaders preach by example. People take their cues from what their leaders do, not what they preach.
- Human Resources (HR) systems need to be aligned to support the vision and values of the organization. Among others, performance appraisals and compensation systems must be aligned to evaluate and reward people based on what the firm really wants to accomplish.
- Managers and leaders must be recruited or promoted based on their ability to implement the stated vision of the firm, and to demonstrate in a tangible manner the organizational values that have been communicated to the organization.
- The financial plan including budgets must be aligned to support the vision; otherwise, people won't take the vision seriously. The financial plan must factor in the long-term vision, as opposed to simply reflecting short-term financial objectives such as quarterly results.
- Finally, it's critical that senior executives use every opportunity to reinforce the vision and the values of the organization. For most people, the vision statement is somewhat abstract, and they need the message to be repeated several times before it truly becomes second nature.

38

Summary

For many organizations, vision is something understood by a limited number of people, generally those at the top of the organization. As discussed earlier, it's difficult to believe that an organization may realize its full potential while a majority of its associates don't understand where the organization really wants to go. As part of their responsibility to create a shared mindset within the organization, leaders must be prepared to invest a considerable amount of time to create, articulate, and communicate their vision to the rest of the organization. It's a necessary condition to fully engage employees toward realizing the organization's objectives. There's a high reward for those willing to invest the time to do it properly.

Let us make a special effort to stop communicating with each other, so we can have some conversation.
  − Judith Martin, Author

Chapter 6

The Great Communication Challenge

One of the major reasons why many organizations fail to optimize on their resources is the absence of a well-articulated and well-organized internal communication strategy. Some organizations do a very good job in every aspect of internal communication. Others don't communicate enough, at the right level, the messages aren't sent by the right people, or lack the appropriate substance, or in some cases, there may be so much communication that employees can't decipher what's relevant to them.

We'll look at various ways to optimize employee communication by examining the reasons why communication is so important, who are the proper message bearers, how to best communicate, and the payback for good communication.

Why does it really matter?

For most people, the answer is pretty obvious. People need to know what's happening and what the company wants to achieve if they're to contribute what's expected of them. In broader terms, a well-organized internal communication strategy is required to create the ideal mindset within the organization. People need to understand what the organization stands for, the vision of its leaders, and the set of values that reflects the way the company wishes to operate.

Beyond that, good communication is required to avoid waste within the organization. Running a large company is rather complex, and there's nothing more wasteful than when employees from different divisions or departments operate at cross-purposes with their peers from other areas. Last but not least, employees need a sense of belonging. They need to feel that they're an integral part of the success of the organization. They need to develop a sense of pride for the organization they work with and represent when dealing with external stakeholders.

Who should own the communication process?

One of the most critical steps in setting up an efficient internal communication mechanism is to determine accountabilities for internal communication. Early on when I was heading a mostly autonomous organization with several lines of business and several staff functions reporting to me, I assumed that communication would take place in one form or another. We had a whole slew of publications, other written communications, quarterly and annual meetings, divisional and departmental meetings, and so I assumed we were doing enough. However, employee surveys didn't always demonstrate the results I would've expected.

At some point, I concluded that I needed to assume greater responsibility for the process. It didn't mean I had to do more myself; in fact, I may have ended up doing less. However, I played a greater role in setting up a more formal internal communication function and assigned specific responsibilities to make sure communication was taking place in an organized fashion. I also played a role in ensuring that we had a more comprehensive view of all communication taking place within the organization. Most importantly, I made sure we had more formal processes to replace a variety of ad hoc efforts that failed to yield the expected results.

One of the most important decisions was to put the HR and internal communication functions under one umbrella. We were looking at HR as an enabler of our human capital strategic capabilities, and it was felt that orchestrating and coordinating the process of communicating to our employees was part of their overall mandate. In several organizations, the internal and external communication functions are combined under one area. I'm sure it can work under that arrangement. Our experience was that we had more success by placing internal communication close to HR.

A major challenge for senior management at all levels is to try to understand what the average person in their organization really understands. It's very common for senior people to have a fairly incomplete view of this. The end result is that they overcommunicate, undercommunicate, use a language that is at too high a level for people to understand what they're talking about, or too basic for the needs of their organization. Having internal communication people closely linked to various parts of the organization is a good way to make sure that what's communicated and how it's communicated will meet the needs of the target audience or, generally, the needs of several different audiences within the organization.

Then there's the major challenge of determining the best person to send or deliver the various pieces of communication. In some organizations, everything seems to come from the top. My own preference was to be pretty selective as to which messages I delivered myself or under my signature, and what I left to other people. I was very concerned that if too many messages came from me, people would get in the habit of pressing *Delete* before the message was read. So I tried to reserve my signature for messages I considered to be in line with the type of messages that should come from someone at my level of responsibility. Generally the preference was to leave messages as close as possible to the originator of the communication (with the VP HR for HR issues, VP Finance for financial matters, etc.). Sometimes for formal staff meetings, we liked to use different people to deliver messages, even if the message being delivered may not have been in their primary area of responsibility. For example, we sometimes used heads of operational divisions to deliver messages of general interest. It helped give a broad exposure to members of the senior team. It also conveyed a sense of teamwork at upper levels, and this became contagious at lower levels as people realized messages didn't change as they talked to different people.

Finally, there's the issue of how to deliver written or verbal messages. There was always a dilemma between delivering everything centrally from the top versus sending everything through the proper operational channels. The risk of sending everything centrally from the top is that of disenfranchising people in middle management. The risk of sending everything through the proper operational channels is that people may be receiving different messages, not receiving messages at the same time, or even worse, not receiving them at all. The compromise we reached was to use the cascading approach; we would send an advance notice to middle management regarding the message that was being sent with some explanatory notes and the expected release time of the communication, and would then enlist their help to answer any questions that their direct reports might have.

How to communicate?

A lot of material is available on the art of communication. I'm not a communication expert myself; so what follows is simply an attempt to outline some principles based on practical operational experience acquired in a variety of senior roles. Generally we tried to promote these guidelines:

- Communication has to be honest; otherwise people clue in quickly to the fact there's no meat to what's being communicated.
- Communication has to be in support of real actions being taken, and those actions have to support communication. People tend to observe what people do as opposed to

what they say, unless they realize that both words and actions are closely connected.

- Although written and verbal communication should look professional, it shouldn't look overly polished. Sometimes communication that looks or sounds too polished for the audience conveys the impression that the message is being embellished and may reduce its credibility.

- If there's a choice between the messages being polished or carrying substance, the preference is to go for substance. Most of the time I used professional communicators to draft messages. They were good and understood my style preference, so generally there was very little need for major changes. However, there were situations where I felt the message would be better understood if I wrote the communication myself as there were some situations that required that type of personal communication. So sometimes substance should prevail over form.

- Speed and timeliness are critical. Some organizations produce good communications but are sent way after their point of relevance – so they don't get read. Speed may be a major asset to help create a sense of urgency within the organization. If communication happens within hours of an event, then people get the feeling rather quickly that the organization is living in *real time*. A few years ago, a division I was heading was involved in trying to acquire the largest contract we had ever quoted on. Within 24 hours of the finalist presentation being made, a bilingual communication went out to all employees explaining the nature of the contract, the process being followed, an update on the previous day, and next steps. At the time, we were trying to create excitement and a greater sense of urgency. It turned out we were eventually awarded the contract, and I'm convinced that this single timely piece of communication was a major contributor in reshaping the culture of the organization.

- It's always a difficult issue to determine the right amount of communication. It's probably more an art than a science, and is very dynamic as the right answer today may not be the same as the right answer down the road. However, you have to be conscious of the fact that there are dangers in both under and overcommunicating.

- When communicating to a wide audience with a diversified background and level of experience, my preference is to aim at the 80th percentile or so, hoping that the communication will be at the right level for 80% of the audience. For half of the rest, they'll get initiated to something new and will gain a better understanding the next time the topic will come up. Then there's always a minority that is difficult to reach, despite our best efforts.

- For organizations operating in all of their official languages, it's critical that communications be available in all languages at the same time. Sometimes logic might indicate that the more expedient way to do it is to release whatever is ready when it's ready. However, it's not a practice likely to be acceptable.

- As a last measure, in case our regular systems failed, we had a tool called ACTION, which was an e-mail tool for anyone in the organization to reach me if they couldn't obtain a satisfactory answer elsewhere. Obviously, this couldn't be the primary communication channel; however, it was a great back-up system for when people couldn't cut through the bureaucracy to get answers.

Summary

For most organizations, internal communication is a critical element to achieve success. There's a high payback for those who do it well. Coordinated and timely internal communication can be a great tool to create the right culture. Communication can also have a multiplier effect, good or bad. The individual or group who is the recipient of a good message from a senior executive will be quick at spreading the word. Soon, people think this is happening all the time, even though it may be happening infrequently. And finally, like anything else, communication efforts have to be monitored continuously to ensure that at the end of the day, they produce a positive return. Results need to be commensurate with the effort being invested.

Profits aren't an option, they're a necessity. Although they are
the last item of an accounting statement, they are just as important,
and just as necessary a cost as any other cost item – wages, taxes, materials,
rents.
  – Ian Sinclair, Former Chairman, Canadian Pacific

Chapter 7

Bringing Financial Focus Deep Within the Organization

In Chapter 2, we identified the lack of financial focus among many employees below the most senior levels of the organization as another important source of leakage. The purpose of this chapter is to address this issue, understand why there's a disconnect, and discuss some of the practical aspects involved in strengthening financial acumen among employees. Although this chapter is written in the context of for-profit organizations, many of the same principles being discussed here also apply to non-profit organizations and government agencies. Obviously, for these organizations, the challenge is somewhat different as the concept of revenues to balance expenses isn't always applicable.

Why is this an issue?

Recall the following narrative from Chapter 2 which describes factors for lack of performance in organizations:

> **Financial focus.** Small enterprises quickly understand the basics of finance. Revenues must exceed expenses by

some margin and positive cash flow is most desirable. This financial focus gets lost as organizations grow. Eventually, except for a few people, employees tend not to see the whole financial picture, and eventually assume that managing the financial aspect isn't part of their job.

Essentially the issue is that while most companies want to engage their employees in achieving their objectives, this is a difficult task when only a limited number of people have a proper understanding of the financial drivers affecting the organization's results.

Admittedly, money isn't everything. However, regardless of the type of organization, money is pretty important, and generally those who forget this fact are quickly reminded there are always financial constraints.

Why is there a disconnect?

There are several reasons why there's a major gap between the company executives' level of financial awareness, and the knowledge of the average person in the rest of their organization:

- Most people don't have a very good financial background and so don't understand financial statements.
- Except for a limited number of employees, people don't understand the magnitude of the numbers reported at the company level. Coming from the financial sector, we often dealt with assets in billions of dollars, profits in hundreds of millions, and expense items at the

department level in the hundreds of thousands. Quite frankly, a lot of people didn't know which was which. For executives, it's mind-boggling that people would confuse these; however, reality is that people do confuse numbers that look straightforward to executives.

- Sometimes people are told that the company isn't doing well, and then they read that the company has made large profits in a given year, say $1 billion. What the executives are saying is that they targeted 20% more than $1 billion. What the employees are seeing is a very large number which seems to be close enough to whatever the target was.

- Sometimes the company announces that the results are below expectations and the stock price might be down, and then they read that senior executives have pocketed large bonuses or have made financial gains on their stock options. Then they can't understand how these two conditions can exist at the same time.

- Often people are told that budgets are cut or frozen because the company results aren't satisfactory. Usually there are deeper reasons why budgets may be cut. It may be to protect credit rating, preserve cash, etc., which obviously have very valid business purposes and are very logical reasons. However, the message isn't always communicated in a manner such that people can really appreciate what their leaders have in mind (the logic they're following). Sometimes the reasons can't be communicated; usually better communication could take place without disclosing deep secrets.

- Recent scandals in some companies and huge write-offs that companies take from time to time to correct the past (such as reducing previously inflated results) also contribute to creating scepticism and confusion among employees. They question what these numbers really mean.
- The further away people are from a true profit and loss centre, the more difficult it is for them to feel a sense of ownership as the tendency is to see financial issues as somebody else's problem. In the absence of having a full picture of revenues and expenses, people focus on their budgets and come to believe that managing a budget is like managing a business.
- The recent tendency of grouping people by functional specialty pushes an increasing number of people away from some kind of bottom line. This means that organizations are further divided between people who generate revenues and those who incur expenses. The end result is that bottom lines are pushed closer to the top of the organization and in the absence of pure bottom line accountability, more people are being micromanaged from the top. This results in more people being disconnected from the reality of running a business as there's little ownership of financial numbers, except at the very top.

Practical ways to strengthen financial understanding and buy-in among employees

Improving the sense of financial ownership over a large base of employees isn't an easy task. Sometimes it may be daunting as typically progress doesn't happen overnight. However, this isn't an excuse for not trying hard to spread financial accountability within the organization. Here are some things you can do to improve the situation:

- Regardless of the type of organization you're dealing with (government, private/public companies, etc.), there are financial drivers that matter to the organization. These need to be explained to employees in basic terms (how they influence cash flow management, credit ratings, revenue generation, reported earnings, etc.). If people understand these drivers, they may find ways to help management in incremental ways. If they don't understand, then they just perform tasks with no good idea as to what links their involvement to final results.
- All organizations need to increase employee awareness and education on financial matters, and organizations should devote some resources to this.
- Educating people on financial matters isn't a one-time exercise. It requires regular efforts in terms of providing updates on how the company is doing and why it's happening, again to further people's understanding.
- There's great value in having as many people as possible connected to a bottom line that resides close to them. It keeps people focused on the business itself as opposed to functions. For example, if there's a choice between having all application technology people working together in one area versus having them decentralized under operational divisions, my preference has always been for the latter. I'd rather have people thinking of themselves as being part of a business unit that needs to

meet financial targets, as opposed to being part of a large functional unit treated as a cost centre without a real revenue stream.

- For incentive compensation purposes, some organizations measure managers by their ability to manage their budget (their ability to underspend). This is wrong. The purpose of the game isn't to save money; it's to apply financial resources intelligently to optimize the spread between revenues and expenses. I've seen groups of people agree very quickly on the need to spend on a certain item or project, and then spend most of the time discussing which budget should assume the expense. This is not a money-making activity and not the way business was meant to be run. Typically, my preference has been to have fewer budgets and eliminate budget savings from the incentive compensation targets. Related to this, I've also seen managers take their people out of required training, again with the view to save on budgets, contrary to the greater good of the organization. The message here isn't that reckless spending should be encouraged. However, *budget* management shouldn't be confused with *business* management.

- Every opportunity should be taken to encourage people to think and act like an owner. Generally when people came to me for spending approval, my first reaction would be to ask them if they would go ahead with the expenditure if *they* owned the company. This helped to simplify the arguments. (Is it required? Why? Do we have the money? What will it do to the earnings picture? etc.). As a side note, thinking and acting like an owner isn't quite the same as thinking and acting like a shareholder, as shareholders aren't a uniform group with well-aligned views and objectives. Owners, as a group, tend to be more closely aligned in their way of thinking. See Chapter 21 for additional comments on this topic.

- In line with the previous point, companies who run their business as a going concern as opposed to running it from quarter to quarter stand a better chance to enlist their people to help them manage the financial aspects of the business.

- One way to engage people to run a good business from a financial standpoint is to have organized processes for people to contribute their ideas toward elimination of wasteful practices, reports that are no longer required, and improvement in process. When asked, people tend to respond well to these initiatives.

- Having executives preach by example is also a necessary condition to engage people toward financial management of the business. There's nothing worse than having messages going out to employees only to be contradicted by the behaviour of senior management. People understand quickly what the real message is.

- Finally, when possible, it's helpful to create a sense of ownership by facilitating broad stock ownership or having profit-sharing arrangements. I see these tools as a step in the right direction to encourage people to become keenly interested in the financial results of the organization. However, this isn't enough for most people, as people still need to gain a better understanding of how their day-to-day actions are linked to consolidated results.

54

Summary

For most people, business financial management isn't something they're familiar or comfortable with because of a lack of exposure to the full picture. So one of management's responsibilities is to make sure they do everything possible to educate their people continuously on this aspect of the business. This is a critical element toward creating a shared mindset within the organization. If management treats its employees like intelligent people, and communicates with them continuously in a clear, honest and open manner, there's a better chance people will become engaged in helping to run the business. In the long-term, this is a high-leverage opportunity for any organization.

Bad things happen when good people sit on their hands. Good things happen when everyone tries to make a difference. These clichés are true.
  – Bob Rae, Former Ontario Premier

Chapter 8

Team Approach – How to Make the Total Exceed the Sum of the Parts

I find it difficult to believe it has taken me seven chapters before I tackled this topic, as I've always considered the team approach to be one of the key success factors within any organization. There are probably a couple of reasons why it has taken me so long to get here. First, it's a difficult topic to explain in a way that can add value (it's difficult to offer a tangible action plan that people will feel comfortable applying). Second, and more importantly, I see the team approach as a final target as opposed to a starting point, as it represents the result of several multifaceted and coordinated actions. It's comparable to a report card. It's something you can only observe long after you've invested a lot of energy and effort – not something you can aim for during the initial stages in any leadership role.

Why is this a critical element of organizational performance?

There are several reasons why promoting a team approach makes a lot of sense. Going back to a simple law of physics, it's a well-known fact that forces being applied in the same direction produce a more optimal outcome than forces that are misaligned. I also believe that individual performance can be enhanced when people feel part of a well-performing team and feel peer pressure to perform at a high level. I'm also a strong believer that individuals who are part of a group with good team spirit will be more creative, as they're looking for ways to make things happen as opposed to finding reasons to create obstacles.

In this chapter, we'll see that creating team spirit only makes sense in the context of creating enhanced team performance and improved results. It's important to appreciate there may be groups with very high team spirit who may not be performing well, as the team spirit may be used for the wrong purposes. So team spirit only matters in the context of being used as a tool to achieve better results in a highly focused work environment.

How does team spirit get created?

Team spirit is a key element required to have a successful team approach. To create team spirit, there are a number of steps required:

1. A clear vision that is communicated and understood by the team, however large or small.
2. Regular communication with the team so people understand what's happening, why it's happening, and feel they're part of the team.
3. Hire people who are comfortable operating in a team environment. Accept the fact that you require different types of people within the team and that people will

bring different attributes to the table. Like a sports team, not everybody can be a superstar in the more visible roles, but everybody can be one in the role assigned to them.

4. Review continued employability of people who have problems operating in a team environment. It's always difficult to terminate people with obvious talent. However, at some point the manager needs to assess the price the organization is willing to pay to have someone operating outside the team.

5. It's critical to send the message loud and clear that priority is given to the team as opposed to specific individuals. It's also critical to reinforce this message through tangible action.

6. Communicate that you expect team members to think one level above where they are in the organization. People should be expected to think about issues as if they were in their boss' shoes. This helps to reduce *insular*-type thinking.

7. Set *team* objectives, not just individual ones.

8. Align incentive compensation with the ideal team approach.

9. Create a sense of ownership among team members. It's difficult to have people think in terms of team approach when the manager appears to own every important issue.

10. Success is contagious. Use every opportunity to remind people of collective successes, especially when the team had to meet major challenges and did so successfully.

11. Last but not least, create a fun environment where people can work hard together but also have fun. It's amazing how people who can have fun together may perform even

better as a team. Just having fun isn't the goal; rather, the goal is to have fun and transfer the sense of team approach into real-life work situations.

Obstacles to the team approach

Unfortunately, team spirit is much easier to destroy than create. There are a number of potential obstacles that managers need to recognize to create a successful team approach:

- Sometimes compensation may stand in the way of successful team creation. As an example, incentive compensation programs that reward individual performance may be an impediment to a successful team approach. People will tend to focus where the rewards are going to be.
- Some organizations choose to organize by function as opposed to along business lines. Organizational design per se shouldn't be a major obstacle; however, it's difficult for people to be team focused when results are measured too far away from the unit. To be successful, teams need to be empowered, and the more disperse the accountability, the more difficult it is for teams to feel empowered.
- Outsourcing of functions may also become an obstacle, but doesn't have to be. However, if outsourcing takes away some of the control, it may be more difficult to empower the team and make it operate on a team-based approach.

- Internal politics tend to kill team spirit. People either believe in a team-based approach or they don't. The more politics the organization is willing to tolerate, the more difficult it'll be to convince people to truly believe in a team approach.

- Sometimes teams are defined at too low a level. Ideally, you'd like people to consider their team to exist beyond their immediate co-workers. Depending on the level of their job, it's better to have people consider their team to be a department, division, or the whole company, as opposed to just their immediate co-workers.

- Company mergers may become a huge obstacle to operating in a team environment. First, mergers generally produce several casualties. People become trained to survive on an individual basis (they need to keep their job first). So the team concept gets downgraded to a lower level of importance. Second, mergers bring together people who may have little desire to work together due to different prior cultures. One of the points being missed in many merger assessments is the negative shareholder value created by soft factors such as a reduction in people's willingness to work as a team, and the resulting confusion and reduction in operational effectiveness.

- Lastly, some managers believe they can get the maximum out of their team members by creating adversity within the group, the idea being that people will increase their performance in the face of adversity. My experience has been that this type of adversity is more conducive to the creation of internal politics than to team performance enhancement.

Some additional tips to make this work

These elements also deserve consideration:

- Team building requires leadership. Sometimes leadership will come from the top. Sometimes you may be fortunate enough to have natural leaders within your team who will be instrumental in creating a great team environment. At the very least, a good manager will recognize this, and make sure these natural leaders are being supported and rewarded.
- The most successful teams are often those that feel empowered (they understand their boundaries and accountability). This won't happen by accident. It's the leader's role to make sure these are defined, communicated and understood.
- Finally, remember that actions are more powerful than words. What you say won't matter if it's not supported by action. Also remember that team spirit is much easier to destroy than to create.

Summary

It's important to remember that team spirit can't be mandated. Team leaders at any level can create the right conditions and hope all the right elements are in place to make sure it happens. If it doesn't, the leader needs to revisit the basic elements and see why not. Sometimes the painful conclusion is that the problem is at the top – the leader himself or herself may be the problem!

Chapter 9

The Suboptimization of Optimization by Function

Optimization by function is the result of a certain management style which promotes the idea of optimizing every function performed in the organization. This management model often leads to another form of organization model which may conflict with how efficiently teams operate, including how empowered employees are. I've included this chapter between Chapter 8 (which deals with team approach) and Chapter 10 (which discusses empowerment) as it impacts both to a certain degree.

Every corporation must decide how to best organize specific functions within its organizational structure. At one end of the spectrum, very small organizations have little choice but to have several functions performed by the same person, as sometimes there may be only one person in the organization. At the other end, very large corporations have a variety of choices as to how to best position specific functions within the organization. Companies may choose to have small units perform several functions, such as application software development and accounting, as part of their overall mission. Alternatively, they may choose to extract all functions that appear to be common to several units, and move these to one area specialized in that specific function. Then this area services all units or a subset of units within the corporation.

Every organization has to decide on the optimal mix for all common functions. It'll vary depending on the needs and characteristics of the organization, and may need to evolve over time. For some organizations, the mix of centralized versus decentralized functions has moved too far in the direction of centralization.

This chapter reviews examples of centralization decisions being made, the appeal for greater centralization, the reasons why centralization may not always be as optimal as it appears, and how you should decide what's right for your own organization.

Examples of centralization versus decentralization

For the purpose of the following examples, let's assume a three-level structure, such as the *company* level, *divisions* representing the major operating units and support areas such as Finance and HR, and lastly *departments* representing functions within divisions.

Example 1 – Technology: Most organizations tend to provide architecture and network support at the company level. However, application software development and maintenance support may reside at the department, division or company level. Sometimes organizations move this function to the company level to gain greater efficiency.

Example 2 – Shared services: Many organizations have moved to a shared service model, sometimes on a national basis, and quite often on a continental or global basis. Again, the logic behind this is that greater functional centralization will lead to greater efficiency and lower costs.

Example 3 – Outsourcing: This has existed for a long time. However, over the last few years, we seem to have witnessed an increasing trend toward outsourcing major functions such as software development, network support, and entire HR transactional functions. In many cases, the basis for such decisions may be a desire for greater efficiency that'll be reflected in short to mid-term savings through very appealing financial arrangements.

The appeal for greater centralization

There are several reasons why organizations choose to centralize functions to a greater level than they already exist. Several of these reasons may be quite legitimate and may result in real efficiency gains, while some of the reasons may be more open to challenge:

- **Greater efficiency**. Essentially, the belief is that by moving specific functions under one specific individual, this function will be performed much more effectively than if the function resided under several individuals who may be wearing several hats.
- **Greater uniformity**. By having the same function such as technology delivered under one organizational umbrella, it may cause greater uniformity in process and tools.

- **Easier training**. Again, by having the same function performed by one part of the organization, it's felt that it'll be easier to put together training programs that can be better leveraged than if each department or division has to train its own people.

- **Greater access to professional development opportunities**. In many organizations, professional people believe they may have greater opportunities if they work in large departments with several similar people. This would be true of finance, technology, legal, actuarial and HR staff, among others.

- **Greater control**. Many people believe it's easier to control quality through centralization of as many processes as possible, and by assigning responsibility of that function to a division head responsible for delivering that specific function.

- **Cost savings**. Last but not least, an important driver for centralization is the appeal for real or assumed cost savings due to some of the factors listed above, but mostly short and mid-term savings.

Why optimal isn't always optimal

There's no argument that some level of centralization is required. The issue isn't whether centralization is desirable but whether *excessive* centralization may be hurtful to the organization, despite the obvious appeal for greater centralization.

Several factors explain why some of the centralization decisions are made for the wrong reasons:

- Typically, functional decentralization involves double-line reporting to a divisional boss and a functional boss. Not everybody can evolve in this environment.

- Linked to the first factor, heads of functional units such as technology, legal and finance, may prefer to have maximum control, and may therefore resist sharing the power with heads of operational divisions and functional heads within these operational divisions.

- Typically, better rounded people are required to operate in a decentralized environment (managers and workers need to have a better understanding of diversified disciplines than under a functional centralized model where depth of functional expertise is favoured).

- It's easier to measure the functional improvements created through centralization than to measure the inefficiencies created by the additional complexity of integrating various functions within a centralized organizational model.

Centralization decisions sometimes ignore these factors:

- A decentralized model tends to favour greater team accountability; accountability resides closer to the people performing the work.

- Decentralized models tend to foster greater creativity (people can see their way through implementing new ideas more easily). Points of decision tend to be fewer and closer to the action. Theoretically, the organizational model should make no difference when it comes to creativity. However, my past experience indicates that it makes an *enormous* difference, although few people can measure it let alone understand it, so it tends to be ignored.

- Centralized models sometimes ignore the fact that clients are looking for greater integration as opposed to optimal efficiency by function. Clients tend to favour single points of contact with single points of accountability. Centralization sometimes goes against this flow. Centralization doesn't automatically result in lesser client integration. However, depending on the fluidity of the organization, it often seems to result in greater difficulty in integrating delivery to clients.

- People often minimize the difficulty involved in integrating the various elements required to shape an organization into a uniform mindset or way to approach situations. For operational divisions, multiplying the number of points of contact outside their own organization will often result in additional points of friction. It's only natural that dealing with functionally centralized units, shared service units, or external outsourcers will increase the likelihood that some of these functional units won't be aligned in priorities, attitude, responsiveness, etc. There's no argument that some or all units outside the division can be well integrated with operational divisions; however, there are more organizations who claim to be able to achieve it than there are who can effectively do it.

Summary

How much decentralization is right for your organization? Obviously, there's no universal answer to this question. The answer will always depend on the state of your organization, its history, and its human and technological capabilities. It'll also depend on the mindset. For a variety of factors, some organizations have a culture such that centralization doesn't work very well. In others, the reverse may be true.

The proper outcome is that centralization/decentralization decisions should be made with a proper understanding of all the factors involved, not just factors that can be measured with a short-term financial focus in mind. Such decisions can only be made by people at the top of the organization, with appropriate input from the various players involved.

The ability of small groups to stop an activity greatly exceeds
the power of large groups to get something moving.
    – Frank Ogden, Futurologist

Chapter 10

The Power of Empowerment

Although it may sound phonetically funny, one of the most powerful tools at the disposal of managers is the power of empowerment. It's one of the ways managers can really add value to the organization by enlisting large numbers of people to behave as if they owned the company, rather than blindly following orders. Yet many leaders and managers don't understand the true meaning of empowerment, or don't know how to really empower people. Next we'll discuss the concept and practical ways to apply it.

What's meant by *empowerment*?

The dictionary defines the word *empower* to mean *to give power or authority to*; *authorize*. In simple words, it means to transfer the authority to act to somebody else. In a work environment, empowerment is a transfer of authority to staff to make decisions and take initiative to conduct the business more effectively. It's much deeper than simply authorizing people to sign cheques or authorize clearly defined transactions. It has to do with sharing a meaningful portion of the action with other people in the organization. A lot of managers aren't comfortable with this latter part as it's not very well defined; so they have difficulty handling this concept.

What does it take to make people feel empowered?

This requires quite a bit more than just telling people they should feel empowered. Empowering people in a meaningful way requires a lot of hard work and it doesn't happen overnight. Empowerment has to become a way of life in a disciplined environment, where all the players understand their role and their boundaries. To create an empowered environment:

- You need a shared vision and mindset, so people aren't left guessing what the leader expects and is comfortable with.
- One of the key ingredients is that this shared mindset isn't the sole creation of its leader but rather the sum total of everything that's good within the organization, wherever this originates.
- Ongoing communication is required so people understand what's an acceptable range, within a continuum of reasonable solutions.
- People must be made to feel like owners and entrepreneurs despite the fact that large organizations need some amount of structure to operate effectively. People need to focus on results, not just actions.
- For most leaders, empowering people means to be prepared to widen the tolerance zone of what's acceptable. Forcing people to land on a single solution

representing *the* solution favoured by the leader isn't conducive to empowerment.

- There has to be tolerance for some mistakes, especially mistakes made because people are trying hard. It doesn't mean that tolerance should extend to sloppiness. However, mistakes need to be used as coaching opportunities to enhance a shared mindset.

- Empowerment should be looked at as a funnel. Initially, it has to be wider as it's difficult for people to guess exactly the tolerance zone. As people get more accustomed to working together, the tolerance zone should narrow down.

- Empowerment requires reinforcement. When people act in an empowered way, they need to be told you're happy with the way they're acting. This can be a very strong message.

- Lastly, any incentive compensation program must be aligned to support the vision of empowerment, so people are rewarded for running a piece of the business as opposed to following instructions.

The ultimate test or when the rubber hits the road

Most managers I've dealt with are generally supportive of empowering their people and they genuinely try to do it. However, the real test is when people who have been empowered don't deliver in a manner deemed acceptable, or when actions taken don't conform entirely to the views of the leaders. This is typically when you see who can talk about empowerment and who really means it. Here are a few ideas and a real-life example to explain them:

- Empowering people is a bit of a trial and error process. Initially people lack the exposure to determine precisely what's going to be acceptable. So it may not work all the time and may require some adjustment.

- Expecting people to come up with the *only* solution acceptable to the manager isn't empowerment; it's called politics and it's counterproductive. I see solutions as being a range of potential courses of action as opposed to a discrete point. Leaders who don't see it that way are generally not very successful at empowering their people.

- It's important not to confuse empowerment and anarchy. Empowerment isn't a license to act outside generally accepted boundaries, nor is it the authority to disregard what's happening outside the person's primary area of responsibility.

- Empowering people doesn't remove the responsibility to have controls in place; however, controls need to be on results as opposed to day-to-day actions. Needless to say, those results are more than just bottom-line results. It has to include meeting compliance, internal audit reviews, and other internal controls.

When I speak about empowerment, I always have in mind the situation where one of our senior people had discussed the possibility of closing down an area that had been set aside as a lunch area with outside catering. It went from a potential course of action discussed at a management meeting, to an e-mail announcement to all employees with no prior communication to the senior team, including me. I had a friendly chat with the person to determine what happened, and his reaction was that we needed to clarify his area of authority as he felt empowered to do what he did. I was able to retrieve a note where I had specifically requested that any such initiative should follow its own due diligence process and should have a proper implementation plan. So this was a short discussion as this had nothing to do with empowerment. We ended up with a major problem with our employees and were eventually able to get ourselves out of it. That was the easy part; the difficult part was to do it in a manner that would save face for the executive, and wouldn't send the signal that people around me weren't really empowered.

Some additional observations

- It almost goes without saying that you need the right people around you to feel comfortable empowering people; so selecting the right people comes before empowerment.
- If you inherit an operation where people weren't empowered to act under the previous leadership, there may be a reshuffling of the deck. Some very good people will emerge from the group and others who did well previously will struggle.
- Some people can't be empowered. They might say they want to be; however, they may have grown comfortable operating under tight guidelines and can't cope with this new freedom to act.
- If you inherit an organization that hasn't been operating at a satisfactory level, you may need to postpone full empowerment for a while; people selection and cohesive

mindset creation should come first as initially people may be incapable of guessing the right direction and an acceptable range of solutions.

- Sometimes leaders may have to allow actions they may not feel entirely comfortable with to send the right message. A group reporting to me had decided to change their titles to reflect more closely what they did and how they wished to portray themselves in the marketplace. Titles became things like *Chief Imagination Officer* for the VP of Marketing and *Chief Excitement Officer* for the head of the division, etc. I can't say I was entirely thrilled with the idea at first; however, the market loved it because it was different – nonboring titles. But more importantly I wanted to send the message that it was OK for people to be somewhat unconventional in an otherwise very conventional environment, as long as we all understood that meeting business objectives was critical. Titles were just an instrument to get there. In the end, I didn't care what titles were, as long as we performed.

- Although there may be an impression that empowerment operates at the individual level, it's probably even more important at the team level. Empowerment needs to be felt at the individual level; however, it needs to result in greater team empowerment and focus.

- Empowerment works better in nonpolitical environments. In political environments, people are too concerned with watching their backs and avoiding mistakes; reducing politics is almost a must before empowering people will produce optimal results.

- Moving into an empowered type of environment will make some managers feel uncomfortable. Good leaders will likely love it as it'll allow them to leverage their team, but weak leaders may well feel they're losing control and this issue has to be addressed with these managers.
- Finally, empowerment should be looked at as a key ingredient in creating pride. People will feel much prouder of results if they feel they own a piece of the action, as opposed to simply executing somebody else's master plan.

Summary

Managing and leading is a multifaceted undertaking. There are many tools available to leaders to influence how they can optimize the performance of people under their responsibility. There's no single element that can work in isolation from the rest. Empowering people is one of the most powerful ways to obtain performance; however, it requires a lot of other work before it's really effective. It requires the right environment, the right people with the right attitude, a cohesive mindset, good communication, and a group of leaders willing to share a piece of the action. Finally, it requires patience, as this isn't something that'll always produce the ideal results right away. However, there's high payback for those who can use it effectively.

I believe wanting is the most important quality a person can bring to business.
— Jimmy Pattison, Company Founder

Chapter 11

A Non-owner Feeling Like an Owner — Dream or Reality?

Although empowerment and ownership both go hand in hand, I've concluded that one of the sources of leakage within organizations is that many employees don't have a sense of ownership. In large organizations especially, many people feel and behave as if they're dealing with someone else's business, not their own. This is due in part to the fact that people see small pieces of the puzzle and therefore don't feel that sense of ownership. So organizations end up with a substantial portion of their people who aren't fully engaged in what they do.

Why is this important to any type of organization?

Developing a sense of ownership among employees is critical as this is the most tangible way that people can align their interests with those of the organization, whether it's a private or public sector organization, privately held or publicly traded. The more people who develop a sense of ownership, the fewer the number of people who behave as bystanders, and the more who'll be willing to roll up their sleeves to get the job done.

Chapter II—A Non-owner Feeling Like an Owner – Dream or Reality?

78

What does it really mean to have a sense of ownership?

People feel they own issues and they own outcomes. They try to make decisions for the right reasons. They take a long-term perspective as opposed to just trying to find expedient ways to deal quickly with issues in front of them. It means they feel like they *own* customers; they value them as if they were their own customers and will handle them accordingly. It also means people will spend the money available to them as if it were their own; they would exercise their best judgement on where and how to spend the organization's money.

What does it take to create an environment where employees have a sense of ownership?

Developing a sense of ownership in an organization is neither an easy nor straightforward task. You can't order people to develop a sense of ownership. Essentially, senior managers within the organization need to create the right environment and encourage people to develop it. There are several elements that need to be present to create this culture of ownership:

- A vision needs to be created and communicated to the organization so people know where the organization wants to go. It also needs to be reinforced continuously.
- There needs to be ongoing communication within the organization so people will understand more than just the piece they're responsible for.
- There has to be strong leadership so people feel they're part of an organization that knows where it's going.

- There has to be a shared mindset and cohesiveness in the organization; otherwise people may feel they have a sense of ownership, but it may produce results that are incompatible with the objectives of the organization.
- Senior people need to be able to share a piece of the action, not decide everything themselves; otherwise people will feel and behave like employees. In other words, it's hard to own a piece of the action if it's already entirely owned by the boss!
- People must have some control or ownership of their time so they can use it as effectively as possible, within certain defined constraints, for the greater good of the organization.
- People must feel valued for who they are and what they bring to the organization. It's difficult to expect to develop a sense of ownership if the organization doesn't make people feel valued.
- Decisions that affect people's work need to be made quickly. Some organizations are very slow at making decisions. So it's difficult for people to develop a sense of ownership when they need to ask for frequent permissions that take forever to be processed.
- Finally, where incentive compensation programs exist, they need to be structured to encourage people to develop a sense of ownership.

Some of the reasons why many people don't develop a sense of ownership

We've dealt with the positive factors that need to be present in the organization to maximize the chance that people will have a sense

Chapter 11—A Non-owner Feeling Like an Owner – Dream or Reality?

80

of ownership. Almost equally important is the need to remove the obstacles or factors that'll impede the objective of the organization in developing a culture of ownership. Some of the obstacles that need to be addressed include:

- Some people, for a variety of reasons, will never develop a sense of ownership, and it may be necessary to review whether such people should continue to be employed within the organization. The answer may vary depending on circumstances and the contribution from such individuals.
- There are many senior managers who don't want to encourage people to behave as owners as it takes away from their control and/or power base.
- Lack of continuity within the organization, such as frequent merger and acquisition activity, tends to create a climate where people feel paralyzed and therefore become much less proactive.
- Some incentive compensation programs don't reward risk taking but rather the status quo, contrary to what a sense of ownership would typically entail.
- A climate loaded with politics can also be quite negative and counterproductive.
- The existence of an overly pronounced *class system* within the management structure can also discourage people from feeling like owners [they feel that *they* (the executives and managers) own the issues and the problems].
- Finally, a number of factors covered earlier regarding creating an environment conducive to a sense of ownership, can also become an impediment if not

handled properly (poor communication and leadership, slow decision making, and managers second guessing their employees' decisions continuously).

Other observations

Some people equate *sense of ownership* with stock ownership by the employees. This isn't entirely correct. Providing stocks to employees may be reinforcing a culture already promoting the sense of ownership; however, this isn't a substitute for creating an environment that promotes people developing a sense of ownership.

I've had the opportunity to conduct a consulting assignment with a community college delivering post-secondary education in Ontario. This is a public sector organization. Yet, I've met many people in that organization who have developed a sense of ownership despite the fact that there's obviously no company stock to be distributed. They don't own stocks. They own a vision, a commitment, and a passion to do the right thing for their clients – the people who attend college to prepare to face the marketplace. This type of ownership, in my mind, is much more critical than ownership of stocks with limited ownership of outcomes.

Summary

Let's compare the creation of an ownership type of culture to the development of team spirit, which I've covered earlier. This isn't the starting point in developing an organizational framework. Several conditions need to be in place to allow this to happen.

Chapter 11—A Non-owner Feeling Like an Owner – Dream or Reality?

82

Very few organizations ever get to the stage where they have a majority of employees feeling they have a sense of ownership. Sometimes organizations don't get there because they're not patient enough, not stable enough to allow the right conditions to be in place, or don't have a game plan to get there. I strongly believe this is another area where organizations would be wise to invest their energy, as this is a very high point of leverage and an area where many organizations fail to realize their full potential. I'm sure most leaders would agree it would be wonderful if every one of their employees felt like an owner and, even more importantly, behaved like one.

You've got to keep moving. What you're most proud of today is quite likely to be scrapped five years hence.
    – Edgar G. Burton, Merchandiser

Chapter 12

Organizational Pride

During my career, I've been associated with several organizations, both as an employee and a consultant. I've been associated with firms with a very proud tradition that was cherished throughout the organization, and other firms with a real *loser mentality* (people didn't believe the organization could be successful and so, acted accordingly).

Determining whether you're dealing with an organization carrying a lot or a little pride is generally easy. You can talk to a few people around the organization and determine pretty quickly the type of organization you're dealing with. The real challenge is to determine what may or may not have caused the organization to become a proud organization. Once an organization is known to be proud, it becomes self-sustained and you can no longer observe the behaviours that caused it to achieve this pride. You almost need to go back in history to determine events and behaviours that were critical to the evolution of the organization.

Let's explore the various factors, positive and negative, that may determine whether or not an organization becomes a proud organization.

Why does organizational pride really matter?

I'm a strong believer that pride is very highly leveraged. A proud organization will achieve things that may not be possible in another environment. People will go above and beyond the call of duty to make sure the organization won't fail, and to make sure they don't let the organization or the rest of the team down. The corollary is that in organizations where there's a lack of pride, people are much less likely to care and there may be a *losing* attitude that can be very contagious. Once the organization is in a rut, it becomes very difficult to dig it out from this type of mindset.

Here's an example. Back in the 1960s, before free agency and expansion of the number of franchises, the Montréal Canadiens in hockey and the New York Yankees in baseball were both known to carry a very strong winning tradition and were very proud organizations. (Maple Leaf fans, I'm sorry not to mention your Leafs. I believe their success predates my arrival in Toronto by a couple of decades!)

Getting back to the Canadiens and Yankees, it seemed like marginal players always became better when they joined these organizations. Newcomers quickly understood the winning tradition and were continuously reminded they were part of a proud organization and were expected to continue the tradition. I strongly believe there's a close parallel to other types of organizations, business or otherwise. Organizational pride can be created and it can be destroyed. Proud organizations will always outperform organizations that lack pride.

What does it take to create organizational pride?

It would be wonderful if a magic recipe existed to create instant pride within an organization. Unfortunately, this isn't the way it works. Typically, you need time and a number of elements to fall into place for pride to be created:

- Time and patience. This process doesn't happen overnight.
- Strong leadership both from the top and from within the organization. You need enough of the right type of people to turn nonbelievers into believers. People who can *walk the talk*, preach by example, and ignite enthusiasm in others.
- Put a vision in place, have a strong communication program, and create a cohesive entity. People can't be proud to be part of a chaotic, political type of organization.
- It's also very helpful to have people who can act as role models for the rest of the organization; people that employees will be proud to imitate, who can instill pride.
- You also need to be able to create an environment where the only acceptable outcome is to win; an environment that doesn't accept failure and mediocrity as a normal outcome.
- There must be a shared feeling within the organization that collective failure is unacceptable. In many organizations, leaders may feel that way, but they may be unsuccessful or incapable of spreading the same feeling around the organization.

- Finally, you need some luck or the right circumstances. Sometimes luck takes the form of being able to recruit someone who'll make a major difference in mindset. It may also take the form of a trigger event. As an example already mentioned in Chapter 6, I remember a few years ago we had the opportunity to quote on the largest ever insurance contract of its kind. The mindset of the organization had not been very good. It used to be a proud organization, but for a variety of reasons, pride had disappeared. Through selective hiring, we ended up with a stronger group, and when the opportunity surfaced to quote on this major contract, a group of people took it upon themselves to make sure we would win. At some point, we recognized we should make the 1,200 other employees share in the excitement through timely communication after each step. Timely meant 24 hours after each event, not a few weeks later. When we did win the contract, it created a lot of collective pride in the organization. This became the trigger event toward a major transformation within that division, and it marked the return to being a proud organization.

How can collective pride be destroyed?

Creating pride in an organization tends to be a very time-consuming process. However, destroying pride can happen much more quickly. Some of the reasons why pride is destroyed or not created include:

- Poor leadership, communication, and lack of a compelling vision.

- Repeated failures within the organization may create a negative mindset around the organization, and may take a long time to overcome.
- In some organizations, management tends to overrule people on a regular basis. It's hardly a recipe for creating pride when people get the feeling what they produce is never good enough to please the leadership.
- Finally, mergers and acquisitions represent a real danger as far as destroying pride. Typically there aren't enough jobs for everyone. So it creates a mentality of losers and winners. Also, one side of the organization will always *win* as far as taking control, so the other side may well feel like losers. In addition, during the integration period, there's too much to do; so it becomes acceptable to cut corners, provide less-than-excellent customer service, and people start focusing inwards as opposed to outwards. Over time the feeling of pride may well disappear.

Other observations

- Some people confuse pride with arrogance. To me, pride is a good characteristic and can generate a lot of positive energy. Arrogance is generally a substitute for substance and excellence (people believe they operate at a level higher than they're really at). Sometimes over time, pride may become arrogance and it marks the beginning of the decline for the organization.
- Success is addictive; failure is contagious. When an organization gets in a rut and can't get out because it lacks the pride to do so, it may require new blood in the

organization; people who aren't encumbered by past failures.

- Pride isn't something you can buy nor something you can mandate. It needs a lot of hard work and it takes time. In the end, it's something that you earn, once you've taken all the right steps.

Summary

Pride is a very high-leverage tool from an organizational standpoint. Similar to other such tools, you need time and patience to create organizational pride. Once you have a proud organization under your responsibility, half your job is done. At that point, people equate collective failure with personal failure. Rather than pointing fingers when things don't work out or trying to obtain personal recognition when things go well, people feel collectively and jointly responsible for both successes and failures. Taking the time to build organizational pride by using a *back to basics* approach can be very rewarding, both from a personal and organizational perspective.

In the modern world of business, it is useless to be a creative
original thinker unless you can also sell what you create.
Management cannot be expected to recognize a good idea
unless it is presented to them by a good salesman.
– David M. Ogilvy, Author

Chapter 13

Creativity

One of the most cherished attributes in any business environment is creativity. It allows organizations to progress and remain competitive. It may be the difference between being a major player in any given market, and being marginal. Creativity by itself isn't a guarantee of success; however, for most organizations, lack of creativity generally results in mediocrity and slow death.

Creativity is one of those things that can be encouraged but not mandated. It's similar to a sense of ownership and pride. An organization can do everything it can to put the right conditions into place, but can only hope it has found the right recipe for the ideal outcome. That being said, organizations can do a great deal to create an environment that promotes creativity. In fact, I feel many organizations have a lot of untapped creative potential; they don't do as much as they could to leverage themselves.

Ideas don't always come from the top. In fact, many of the great ideas come from within the organization. However, many organizations don't have the proper processes to collect ideas where they exist. Instead they hire consultants to make recommendations. There's nothing wrong with hiring consultants (remember I do this for a living!). However, they should be hired for the knowledge, skills, and experience they already possess, not merely for making recommendations based on ideas that already exist in the organization.

Let's put some framework around this elusive concept of creativity.

What does it take to promote creativity within an organization?

A lot of organizations run their affairs on a project basis. Their business is a mix of ongoing regular activities such as selling and servicing, and less regular activities such as projects to maintain or enhance their products and services. Creativity isn't a project; it should be an ongoing activity. Yet many organizations don't have the proper framework to turn creativity into an ongoing activity. To establish a creative organization, a number of elements need to be in place:

- There should be strong communication so that people understand their environment, the challenges, and opportunities facing the organization. Once people better understand the organization, they can determine more easily how to focus their creativity toward its needs.
- People must feel that their ideas are welcomed and valued. It may help to have creativity formally mentioned

in the core values of the organization; not the complete answer, but it may help.

- Creativity seldom originates from the top of the organization. People at the top may have ideas but often lack the specific knowledge required to turn these general ideas into tangible actions. So people at various levels of the organization need to be enlisted. Management needs to remove obstacles to ensure that creative ideas may be implemented. In terms of removing obstacles, eliminating politics is quite important; otherwise people compete to kill ideas instead of facilitating the implementation of other people's ideas.

- People need to be mentally involved. Politics and poor management practices in general contribute to people looking at their involvement in the organization as a *job* as opposed to a *passion*. People who care about their organization, who are passionate about their environment, are much more likely to be creative.

- People need to be challenged. When people are challenged, they're more likely to find creative solutions. When difficult projects are given to capable people, but people for whom the project may represent a stretch, these resourceful people may come up with amazing solutions.

- There must be processes to collect ideas; otherwise, good ideas go to waste and people stop offering them as they feel they can't make a difference. A direct line to the top may also help. Sometimes, despite management's best efforts, bureaucracy may stand in the way of collecting and implementing ideas. A direct line to the top, electronic or otherwise, may be a tool to ensure people feel there's always a way to be heard.

- Having ideas presented is the primary challenge. Once they're presented, there must be a follow-up mechanism. There must be a formal response provided to people. If employees feel their ideas are ignored, they'll quickly lose interest. Not every idea has to be accepted, but should be followed up. Creativity isn't something that can be turned on and off at will. Management needs to keep the creativity flowing.

- Generally, people offer ideas and creative solutions because they care for the organization. However, it may also help to provide some form of recognition. People like to be recognized, but in addition, recognition sends a signal to the rest of the organization that fresh ideas and creative solutions are important.

How can creativity be destroyed?

As mentioned earlier, there are numerous challenges in setting up the right conditions to promote a creative environment. Destroying creativity is much easier than promoting it, and many organizations do a good job (or a poor job depending on the perspective) in that respect. Some of the factors that may contribute to destroying or inhibiting creativity include:

- Bureaucratic behaviour. Bureaucratic organizations are experts at killing ideas. In general, bureaucratic environments will have approval processes that'll require a dozen or so people to agree before an idea may be implemented. However, one or two people who disagree with the idea is generally enough to kill it. The deck is stacked against creativity. The structure and processes favour the status quo at the expense of creativity.

- Quite often ideas may be generated at lower levels of the organization and passed on to the immediate operational manager. With the delayering of managerial levels that has taken place in several organizations, managers can hardly survive with what they already have on their plate, and have limited appetite for taking on more; so they may provide little incentive to promote creativity within their unit.

- Too many organizations are satisfied with copying ideas from other organizations. Either because they can't generate ideas or because they can't implement them, they start describing themselves as followers or quick followers. Once this mindset becomes embedded in the organization, employees quickly realize that it's not part of their job description to be creative.

- Failure to invite new ideas from within the organization is a major sin as far as creativity is concerned. However, a worse sin is to ignore ideas when they're presented. People quickly stop contributing ideas once they feel their ideas disappear into a black hole.

Other observations

- A good source of potential creativity is complaints, whether originating from customers, distributors or employees. Not every complaint or criticism is necessarily valid. However, some organizations take the radically opposed view (they don't listen at all). If organizations listen carefully, they may see opportunities to be creative and deal with the sources of their customers' and employees' frustration.

- Customer and employee advisory groups may also be a good source of creativity. Creativity isn't always building from scratch. It's also the ability to link together several known elements and come up with solutions that others may not have contemplated.

- Despite the fact that creativity isn't a project, a one-time project to promote ideas and suggestions may be helpful and may create some excitement. However, this works best if it's part of a new comprehensive strategy being put into place for the future. The issue with an idea blitz is that the volume may be too much to handle at once, and creativity may soon die after the blitz is over.

- Several organizations have suggestion boxes to encourage creativity. I'm sure these can play a useful role. If they work (if people actually use them), then there must be a very disciplined process to screen ideas, follow up with the author, and champion ideas into tangible action once they're accepted.

- Although people shouldn't be discouraged from providing ideas, it's also important that they be encouraged to provide ideas with some logic as to why these ideas will make a difference. Otherwise management people are then forced into doing research to prove or disprove the relevance of the ideas, and this may become very time consuming.

- The types of hobbies and activities some of our employees engaged in outside their regular job have always amazed me. Company magazines often describe how some of their less well-known employees play some very active roles, often involving a lot of creativity, *outside* work. Yet these people aren't known for their creativity *in* the work environment. I don't believe people can be creative at night and not have the potential for being creative during the day. This is simply a reflection that people may be in the wrong job, or more likely their potential isn't fully engaged while on the job.

Real-life demonstration

My daughter spent a few summers working as a summer student in a financial institution, and during one of these summers, the management team asked the small group of summer students to take on a project to revamp the mailing of periodical statements showing clients' financial holdings. Management knew there were issues with the way things had been handled, and for various reasons didn't have time to do a proper review and come up with appropriate solutions. The students had to get organized, review the current procedures, and present recommendations through a formal verbal presentation to the management team.

The management team was very impressed with the creative solutions presented, and they ended up being implemented for the most part. Management didn't generate these ideas. They generated the proper environment and challenged a group of people to think outside the box. They were well rewarded for it.

The division to which my daughter had been assigned was likely the most creative organization I've observed during my career. There was a culture of creativity. This is a very small sample of what this organization was able to accomplish over the years using its creative mindset. However, they had only reached this point after several years. So the organization was reaping benefits after several years of hard work focused on creating the right environment.

Summary

Destroying creativity is much easier to do than promoting it. In earlier chapters, I've made reference to losses of potential within organizations. The absence of a creative environment is a primary example of how organizations can fail to reach their real potential. Organizations may contribute greatly to their future success by nurturing an environment allowing their creative people to be challenged, valued and rewarded.

No one in history ever went forward by taking steps backward.
   – Jean Drapeau, Long-time Montréal Mayor

Chapter 14

The Focus on Focus

I've had the opportunity to be associated with a large number of organizations. I've always been struck by the wide difference that exists between organizations when it comes to focus. Some organizations are really good at determining what they want to achieve and getting organized to get it done. Others seem to be all over the map. They have grandiose plans on paper and spend a lot of time talking about what they want to accomplish, but spend little time organizing the execution of their plans. At the end of the day, this all amounts to organizational discipline or focus, or a lack thereof.

Why is focus so important?

Managing large (or not so large) organizations is a difficult task under the best of circumstances. People show up to work with different backgrounds, ideas, agendas, etc. In the absence of a proper framework, it's unlikely that people are going to work in a coordinated way. Every organization has limited resources and generally an infinite appetite for new projects. So it's critical that available resources be used at their optimal level and that leakage of potential be reduced to a minimum. One good way to eliminate leakage is to ensure the organization is very focused on what the objectives are, and how they can be executed.

A high-level view of the conditions required to create focus

It won't come as a surprise that management has a critical role to play in keeping the organization focused. In fact, this is what management is paid to do (provide general and specific directions as required, ensuring the organization is focusing on these directions, and is executing the agreed-upon strategy). It sounds pretty simple but many organizations fail to do this and employees continue to do what they think they should do. To create focus, I believe a number of high-level conditions need to exist:

- Strong leadership and management capabilities in the organization.
- Management that gets involved, understands the issues, and can lead in setting priorities.
- A cohesive team that understands the issues facing the organization at large, can elevate itself above the team's immediate concerns, and determine priorities from an overall organizational standpoint. In other words, you need a management team whose members can elevate themselves one notch above their area of immediate responsibility.
- You need good communication within the organization to create a shared mindset to minimize conflicting agendas and timetables.

- Although this may sound simplistic, a game plan needs to exist (a strategic plan and an operational plan). In other words, it's easier to focus on the plan if one really exists and is understood by the various stakeholders.

- There must be some continuity in the organization. Ongoing changes of executive and management staff is very detrimental to focus. People must be in their jobs long enough to execute the game plan, be accountable for their decisions, and learn from mistakes so organizational focus can continue to improve.

- Mechanisms must exist to allow new projects to get approved; equally important, there must be mechanisms to review ongoing projects and take them off the agenda if their existence can no longer be justified.

- Finally, mechanisms must also exist to approve new product and service initiatives; however, many organizations fail to have similar mechanisms to eliminate products and services that are no longer required or justified. Many organizations continue to pile up products and services on top of existing ones, and can no longer focus on what really matters due to an ever-increasing volume of products and services that need to be managed.

Specific tools that can be used to stay focused

Assuming an organization has a proper general approach to allow it to focus on the right priorities, there are specific tools and actions that can help keep an organization focused:

- Insist on seeing properly documented realistic business cases to make sure that people have thought their projects through.
- Once projects are approved, insist that they be managed according to proper project management techniques.
- Set reasonable deadlines and have people stick to them.
- Insist on seeing tangible deliverables on a regular basis and celebrate when deliverables occur. Having several short-term deliverables as opposed to one long-term deliverable seems to work better for a variety of reasons.
- Set up a project review group, independent of the project team, to review projects across the organization and make sure people are being kept accountable for their promises. In a previous job, we had this type of cross-divisional *major project* review committee, and I believe it added significant value to the organization.
- In my experience, one of the areas requiring the most help in setting priorities is Information Technology (IT), responsible for software maintenance and development. This area can quickly become unfocused in the absence of strong guidance as far as setting priorities that meet business needs.
- Another area requiring help and attention is Product Development. It always appears this area has more ideas, offered to them or generated by them, than they can realistically execute. Unfortunately, they sometimes appear to pursue too many of these ideas at once, reducing the focus required to have a major impact.
- Finally, when an incentive compensation program exists, it should be applied to ensure people focus their efforts

where the organization wants them to focus. A lot of incentive compensation programs attempt to accomplish too much, and as a result, contribute very little to focus the organization where it matters.

Impediments to focus

There are a number of factors that may become obstacles to an organization's ability to focus on its most important objectives. The conditions we discussed earlier are critical to creating focus. If they're absent, they become an obstacle to creating it. In addition, these factors may also be obstacles:

- Internal politics which cause people to be distracted from the real agenda, or people who manipulate the logical agenda to accommodate their personal one.
- In the absence of managers and leaders determining priorities, people at lower levels will determine priorities themselves. It's both unfair and inappropriate to let people at lower levels decide what the leaders can't. There's nothing wrong with delegation and empowerment when this is a well thought-out approach. However, many organizations create large volumes of work and don't provide the support required to actually complete the work. The result is that people at lower levels decide what they can handle, and then management is critical when their priority work isn't being delivered on time.
- Business cases are a very useful tool. However, some organizations hide behind them to slow down the process and avoid making decisions.

- Many organizations suffer from the *everything is a priority* syndrome. In the absence of thoughtful resource allocation, this is akin to management abdication.
- In sales environments, keeping focused is a challenge. Salespeople can be somewhat unfocused unless there are strong filters in place. People who rely on sales for their livelihood may have a tendency to pursue *opportunities* that make no sense for the organization. This is especially true for services being sold to corporations and where off-the-shelf packages may not always exist. Sometimes management has to step in to ensure that the products and services being sold are the right type for the organization as a whole. Otherwise the organization may become spread too thin because it's too unfocused.

A real-life example

This may help clarify the concept of focus. In one of the organizations I was responsible for, people were complaining that IT wasn't fast enough to produce the required changes to our technology tools. IT people were frustrated because they worked hard but were working on too many priorities. For a variety of reasons, adding resources wasn't a viable option. We brought together the management team that included the head of the division's IT, and it was made clear that we would *not* leave the room until we had a set of priorities that were acceptable to everybody, and could then be communicated to the people executing the work. I would like to say it was an easy exercise – but it wasn't. IT had 10 to 15 major priorities and they all looked like reasonable ones. Essentially we worked from both ends of the priority list (we identified priorities we could eliminate or defer). Then we set a list of *must do immediately* and worked at this until the priority list was balanced with the amount of resources available. At that point, everybody understood this was the best we could do with these available resources, and that *everything is a priority* would no longer work. For the management team, it was a rather tiring session; we had to make choices we'd hoped we wouldn't have to make. However, the exercise turned out to be a rewarding one for the management team and for the IT group. IT could finally focus, and the management team could finally expect delivery on what the IT group had agreed to deliver.

Summary

Keeping an organization focused is always difficult, especially in large organizations with multiple divisions and multiple projects, products and services. The fact it's a difficult task isn't a reason for management not to play its role. A number of organizations fail to provide the proper framework for ensuring people can focus on applying their skills, as opposed to running around in circles. In my view, it's an area where organizations don't invest enough time. I strongly believe there's substantial untapped potential in this area, and organizations that focus on being focused are being well rewarded.

Man is by nature a political animal.
  – Aristotle, Philosopher

Chapter 15

Internal Politics – A Necessary Evil or Disease That Can be Cured?

One of the many reasons why many organizations fail to reach their potential is the presence of internal politics. In general, the question isn't whether politics are present within organizations; rather how much they exist. It would be unrealistic to assume that any organization would be totally immune from it. There are generally several reasons why and how politics exist; however, politics are often ignored and viewed as a necessary evil. Politics don't have to be a necessary evil. There's a cure – once leaders acknowledge it's an issue they can do something about.

What are politics?

Essentially, politics result when the organization fails to align the behaviour of its employees with the interests of the organization, and tolerates the fact that some employees are acting in their own self-interest or in the interest of a part of the organization, at the expense of the rest.

Chapter 15—Internal Politics – A Necessary Evil or Disease That Can be Cured?

106

Politics within an organization can be compared to several forces pulling in different directions as opposed to these same forces all pulling in the same direction. Anyone with some background in physics is aware that forces pulling in the same direction are additive while those pulling in different directions are subtractive. The end result depends on the intensity of the forces at play, how well they're aligned, and how badly they're misaligned.

Realistically, it's difficult to imagine that forces within an organization would always be perfectly aligned. However, it's management's responsibility to monitor the forces at play and jump in whenever these become too misaligned.

At the end of the day, politics are the direct result of a lack of focus and teamwork within the organization. Someone has to take responsibility for it. Generally, accountability starts at the top of the organization, division, or department suffering from misalignment.

As a side note, politics don't only occur in large organizations. It's also amazingly present in very small organizations where there are fewer forces at play, but where the intensity and depth of rivalry can sometimes far exceed what can be observed in larger organizations.

Why do politics exist in organizations?

There are a variety of reasons explaining why politics exist and their intensity within any organization. These can be classified in a number of ways:

Leadership
- Obviously, most issues that exist in organizations can be traced back to some form of failure at the leadership level. It's certainly true of internal politics. I look at politics as the failure of leadership to convince people to set aside their own immediate good for the good of the organization. In the absence of a compelling cause being shown to them, people create their own departmental, divisional or personal cause, and this is what they fight for at the expense of the organization as a whole.
- Politics are also the failure of leadership to sell its vision to the rest of the organization. Obviously, this assumes that a compelling vision exists in the first place. Whether it's that the vision isn't communicated or people don't understand or buy into it, the end result is the same (you have people in the organization not focused on company objectives) and leadership must be accountable for this.
- To have an organization moving in the same direction and performing as a single entity, there needs to be cohesiveness, and for cohesiveness to exist there needs to be a shared mindset within the organization. This is what leadership gets paid to do; create a shared mindset to optimize performance.

Chapter 15—Internal Politics – A Necessary Evil or Disease That Can be Cured?

108

- Interestingly enough, some leaders create internal politics voluntarily by creating tensions in the organization. This is done with the belief that internal rivalry is good to get the best out of people. I suppose it can work in some environments; however, it looks to me like playing with fire. It can be fun, but once the fire is started and out of control, it can quickly become a big mess!

Cultural and organizational issues

- Sometimes politics may be the result of faulty organizational design resulting in lack of clarity and accountability. People end up fighting to clarify what management hasn't yet clarified for them through proper organizational design.

- Sometimes people don't feel empowered and there may be a culture of not accepting mistakes. So people become calculating, avoid taking risks, and make sure they cover their tracks in case something happens. In that type of environment, people are generally quick at blaming each other for mistakes or underperformance, as opposed to focusing on recovering from mistakes and learning from them.

- Closely associated with the previous point, some organizations don't encourage and reward entrepreneurship and creativity; so people learn to become good bureaucrats and survivors as opposed to contributing to their full potential.

- In many organizations there's an imbalance between the so-called *staff* jobs looking after corporate-type functions versus operational functions. People in staff jobs often initiate and/or execute projects that haven't been planned for by people in operations. Then it becomes an ongoing struggle between staff people who are trying to achieve their goals, and operational people who are trying to get out of these unwanted projects and focus on the day-to-day operations. Not surprisingly, one might say this is also a failure of leadership to get everybody on the same wavelength, to avoid having people at lower levels slugging it out in an environment charged with politics.

- Finally, politics should never be discussed without considering incentive compensation programs and their impact on politics. A number of these programs are there to ensure total pay is competitive, but ignore the damage that can be done to an organization when mixed messages are being sent through faulty incentive compensation programs. That is, if these programs are in place, they need to be well aligned with the goals of the overall organization.

Staffing

- Generally politics aren't attributable to specific individuals, but rather to some systemic failure within the organization. Sometimes they're due to the people running the organization and their failure to address the issue. However, it may well happen that certain situations are caused by specific individuals who can't operate in a team environment. This can happen in organizations that focus their recruiting and promotions on individuals with

Chapter 15—Internal Politics – A Necessary Evil or Disease That Can be Cured?

110

good technical abilities at the expense of those with good teamwork abilities.

Communication

- A contributing factor to creating a political environment is the absence of proper communication within the organization. One of the roles of leadership is to replace uncertainty by certainty and to replace confusion with clarity. Generally when people don't know, they assume, and when different people and departments don't make the same assumptions, increased politics are likely to result.

What can be done to minimize politics?

At this point, solutions that can be put in place to minimize politics should be fairly obvious – they should be just the opposite of the behaviours that allow politics to exist. A number of these solutions are explored in this book. Some of the factors required to create an environment with minimal politics are:

- creating and sharing vision
- creating a shared mindset
- hiring people with the right attitude
- having people in leadership positions who can lead and be role models for the rest of the organization
- developing and executing a proper communication strategy
- creating a proper organizational design to serve the best interests of the organization

- aligning reward systems to make sure they support the objectives of the organization.

Summary

Politics are a cancerous disease eating away at organizations. Leaders must be capable of diagnosing the disease when it exists, addressing the root causes, and putting in place appropriate solutions. Ignoring that a problem exists or accepting it as normal isn't what leadership is all about. In most organizations, spending time alleviating the issues that create politics is a good time investment on the part of its leaders.

As my grandfather used to say,"You can do anything you want, but you can't do everything you want."
    – George Torok, Motivational Speaker

Chapter 16

There's So Much to Do and So Little Time to Do It

This sounds familiar, doesn't it? Every time you talk to people in the corporate world, you very seldom hear people complaining about having too little to do. Due to mergers and ongoing restructuring, it always appears that people who are employed have too much to do, and those looking for jobs have a hard time finding one. So for people with jobs, time management is critical to survival.

Much has been said and written about the topic; yet, time mismanagement still seems to be the norm for a lot of people in management jobs. This chapter doesn't attempt to cover everything on this topic. Rather, it's the result of several years spent observing people's work habits.

Why is time management so critical?

In some businesses such as most organizations in the financial sector, expenses linked to people are a major portion of their total expenses. Organizations spend a lot of time optimizing expenses on IT, rent, capital expenditures, etc., but very few do a great job at optimizing how they manage their main expense (the people side of their business). Some people feel it's the employees' responsibility to manage their own time, and if they work 70 hours per week, it's their issue, not management's issue. Obviously, this view doesn't take into account productivity issues linked to people who are mentally exhausted. Nor does it consider people who have to take time off due to burnout and other forms of mental exhaustion.

Unfortunately time management improvement is only possible when individuals who mismanage their time accept they have a problem and are willing to make the change. Most people whom I felt had an issue with time management *could* recognize they had an issue; however, I was mostly unable to have them change their habits except over very short periods of time.

Often time mismanagement at senior management levels is the result of a lack of focus, of ability to make choices and to prioritize, and of ability to truly leverage themselves through the rest of their organization. So time mismanagement may be an indicator of more serious issues in their part of the organization, based on the assumption that the same lack of discipline exists in the rest of their work habits.

The basics of time management – the good

In a nutshell, good time management habits start with creating a game plan, whether documented or simply mental. If people know what they want to achieve, it's easier to allocate their time accordingly. It's also easier to eliminate some activities that fall outside the main game plan. I've divided my observations between desirable behaviours (the good) and undesirable behaviours (the bad and the ugly).

Some of the good approaches:

- Decide what you want to achieve, which activities will take priority, and then fit the rest if time allows; otherwise, don't allow these less critical activities to take time away from you. For instance, if you decide your priority is going to be around financial management of the business, client relationships and employees, then time allocation should be structured accordingly. Activities that don't fall within these three broad types should go way down the list.
- Whether intuitively or more formally, analyze how you spend your time, identify the major sources of time consumption, and determine whether you're happy with the result.
- For most executives and senior managers, there will always be three major sources of time consumption: e-mails, group meetings, and one-on-one meetings. In most organizations, some of these aren't well managed. It's critical that people pay attention to whether these are structured in a way that optimizes people's time. As an example, someone at the VP level mentioned to me she was receiving 300 e-mails per day. I mentioned laughingly that her title should be changed to VP E-mails as this seemed to be enough to consume 100% of her

time. I don't know what the solution is in that specific case; however, the status quo is clearly unacceptable.

- It's important that people make a judgement call regarding the appropriateness of investing time on specific activities in relationship to total time available. As an example, some people not reporting to me directly always tried to book an hour or so to come talk to me about some issue. Sometimes it might be an issue they felt deserved my attention, but in the overall picture it may have been fairly small. So I would ask myself whether the issue deserved 2% of my time in the office for that week. Typically, the answer would be *No* and the meeting would be cut back to 15 minutes, or I would suggest some other way to deal with the issue.

- Early on in my management career, I tried to learn and apply the principle of delegation at the right level. This can help a lot as far as managing time. Also, I learned about upward delegation (people who want to push their responsibilities back to you) and learned quickly not to accept it.

- People in senior management jobs have to learn to say *No* to people who try to consume time that shouldn't be consumed. Typically people look after *their* best interests, and while it may be in the best interests of people to take some of your time, it may not be in *your* best interest to donate time to everybody asking for it.

- In most organizations, there's always pressure for people to take on more than they can reasonably handle. My view is that it's everyone's responsibility to manage their own time and mental health. There are situations that don't make sense and people should look at reorganizing responsibilities to return the situation to a normal status. Sometimes it's outside people's control, but this should be brought up with whoever can fix it.

The basics of time management – the bad and the ugly

There are two ways to improve time management. The first is by following good practices. The second is by eliminating bad ones. In the area of time management, the latter is almost as important as the former. Here are some of the bad practices that need to be reviewed:

- One of the main reasons why people run out of time is because they take on more than they can do. Sometimes it's imposed by circumstances; however, I know plenty of people who like to look very busy for the sake of looking very busy.
- Some people are very efficient – in doing the wrong things. This isn't meant to be funny. It's real. You might be very efficient in reviewing a document or a process – that you shouldn't be reviewing in the first place.
- Some people are chronically overbooked. They feel sick when they see white space in their agenda and look for more to book in their diary. They never learn that things can and do happen all the time, and that white space in the diary allows for dealing with these situations.
- Some people are very efficient at killing fires. In fact they love it because they've become very good at it. For these people, identifying why these fires get started in the first place might be a wise way to spend their time to avoid future crises.

- Lack of proper delegation and empowerment. Some people never find their proper comfort zone and are continuously in and out of issues they probably shouldn't be involved in.

- Micromanagement of issues may also be a major time consumer. Some senior managers never have enough time to do their job, but always have time to get involved in small issues that should be handled by someone else.

- Procrastination (leaving everything to the last minute). Some people need to drop everything all the time to attend to these now urgent issues.

- Lack of proper communication. Time that should've been invested up front is now required in multiples later on as issues arise.

- I've seen people aiming for perfection on activities that don't require the level of perfection being targeted. Some people will refine ad nausea presentations and speeches that nobody will ever remember in the not-so-distant future.

- Feeling obligated to attend every internal meeting or external conference where there might be a chance of relevant content. Some senior managers can't differentiate between *must attend* and *nice to attend* events, so they attend both.

- People must be able to determine whether they can afford the time to volunteer for outside duties such as associations, etc. Obviously there's nothing wrong with volunteering, except if people volunteer at the expense of their primary job.

- Lastly, a lot of people have a so-called *open door policy*. This sounds great in theory. However, it shouldn't mean the door can never be closed, or that anyone can enter at any time to discuss any topic; otherwise when can people focus and get anything accomplished?

Summary

Time is money, and a lot of organizations don't scrutinize time expenses to the same extent as other much smaller hard-cost expenditures. I believe there's a lot of potential leverage for organizations who care to invest time – managing their time!

A committee meeting is where bureaucrats are born,
ideas are killed and the status quo preserved.
    – James H. Boren, Neologist

Chapter 17

The Meeting Mania

In previous chapters, I've noted one factor inhibiting the effectiveness of organizations is the absence of good controls over internal meetings. I'm sure many organizations do an excellent job controlling meetings; however, I've seen several organizations that lack the basic discipline to optimize the time spent in them. We'll summarize the issue, identify some symptoms to watch for, and some tangible actions that can be taken to bring control over financial resources being invested in meetings.

Why is this an issue?

Meetings aren't bad *per se*. In fact, they're a very good way to communicate, arrive at decisions with proper input, and create a shared mindset within the organization. In fact, physical meetings may be much more efficient than virtual meetings over e-mail which may also be very time consuming, create communication issues where none needed to exist, and may not be very effective at dealing with those issues.

The issue with meetings is that in many organizations, they lack the proper structure and discipline that may exist for other activities in the organization. Most companies have pretty clear guidelines for spending authorities when it comes to hard-cost items where a physical disbursement needs to take place. However, when it comes to meetings, many organizations are reckless at accounting for the cost of the meeting and holding people accountable for the results. In reality, every day there may be thousands of dollars wasted on meetings that don't need to take place, that last too long, are attended by too many people, or worst-case scenario, fail to produce any tangible results.

The unspoken feeling is that as long as it's an internal meeting, there's no cost to the organization, as people are paid regardless of the way they use their time. In reality, internal meetings pose a great cost to the organization. Organizations could operate with fewer people in the absence of wasteful meetings. They could be more effective dealing with other issues, or people could simply shorten their workday and be less exhausted from spending long days in the office. If people aren't exhausted, they can be more creative.

Some senior people are so booked up in meetings they have little time to do their job and deal with client and employee issues. For many people, corporate life is an ongoing flow of meetings during the day, followed by a mad rush back to their office to make or return phone calls, late departures for dealing with crisis situations, and evenings or weekends spent catching up on e-mails that have piled up while they were sitting in meetings. So any positive step toward improving management of meeting time is likely to produce a huge incremental impact on the effectiveness of any organization.

Some symptoms that you may have a meeting issue

I'm sure every one of you has been in contact with organizations where people are never reachable. Essentially the answer is always the same – the person is in a meeting. Again, there's nothing wrong with being in meetings. The problem is too many meetings that last too long. If you can cut 25% of the meetings and 25% of the time spent in each meeting, this is a 44% time savings in meetings. Even a 10%/10% reduction (quite achievable) is a 19% reduction in time spent in meetings. So, if you're always in meetings, maybe you don't need to be!

Another symptom that your organization may have an issue with meetings may be obvious if you attend too many meetings where the material isn't organized, people aren't prepared, there are no stated deliverables for the meeting, you never see minutes, etc. A good clue that you have a major problem is when you attend a meeting and people have a problem determining who exactly called the meeting and who is running it. If this has never happened to you, you're very fortunate indeed.

Finally, if you're invited to meetings with no end time, it may be an indication that people have no respect for other people's time and so expect people to keep their schedules open for much longer than required. Again, I've seen this on several occasions, especially in meetings where I had limited control over imposing an end time. As you may guess these were meetings called by more senior people or people from other parts of the organization.

Tangible actions to optimize meeting time

- Tighten up controls over who can call meetings and accountabilities for time spent in them. At some point, I toyed with the idea of asking people to identify the cost of specific meetings based on per hour charges. We abandoned it due to complexity. However, if people had to explain why they incurred a $2,500 charge for a 3-hour meeting, or if their budget were accountable for the expense, I'm sure meeting time and number of attendees would be reduced.

- Have an agenda with beginning and end times for each item. It doesn't mean the meeting has to unfold exactly as scripted; however, it provides a sense of joint responsibility to stay on schedule. I introduced this with a board of trustees with high-level outside board members. At first they thought it was strange, and then they liked it as everyone understood when the meeting had to finish, and it helped plan the meeting content and their departure time.

- Tighten up time allocation and force people to have a clear idea of expected outcome. When running internal management meetings, sometimes we had people from lower down in the organization requesting to cover a specific item in person. Typically they would ask for 45 minutes out of 3 hours. The first step was to ask them to do it in 15 or 20 minutes, and when they came to the meeting I would ask them to state clearly the purpose of their presentation and the expected outcome (information only, request for feedback or immediate decision, etc.). This avoided having chat sessions as opposed to working sessions.

- Have a clock in every meeting room. It seems too simple, but it works. Many people just lose sight of the time and at some point people realize they're out of time; at that point, people start leaving, there's no conclusion to the meeting, and another meeting gets called two weeks later to continue the discussion.

- Send a clear message to people that it's acceptable to decline certain meetings. At some point, we issued meeting guidelines and told people they could decline meetings if they had only a marginal contribution to make, and would use colleagues or minutes to obtain the information they needed. All of a sudden, attendance at meetings started to decline as people started making a judgement on cost of attending versus expected benefits.

An example

In one organization, we had issued fairly detailed guidelines to help people assess the way they conducted meetings and also the need to attend such meetings. I've reproduced here the covering memo which provides a pretty good idea of the message we were trying to send to the organization:

Re: Meeting Management

From: Marcel Gingras

It's said that the only certainties in life are death and taxes – but most of us would probably add *meetings* to that list. While we can't escape the first two items, there's a lot we can do to manage meetings within the organization.

Meetings carry a heavy price tag, both from a financial and a productivity perspective. They cost so much, **per person**, **per hour**, plus fixed costs; and the *productivity lost* costs are equally large. While you're attending meetings, your work is piling up and you can't take phone calls – which means often you work late to play catch-up.

We believe that meetings are an important tool to help us achieve our overall business goals and objectives. As part of our focus this year on improving leadership and management capabilities, the Leadership Team has adopted the following practices to establish consistency in our approach to meeting management:

Philosophy Regarding Meeting Management

- **Be discerning** – about the need for meeting; plan meetings with a purpose.
- **Prepare** – release an agenda 48 – 24 hours prior to a meeting and clearly indicate any advance preparation that needs to be done.
- **Arrive on time** – with advance preparation done, and be ready to participate.
- **Finish on time** – even better, aim to finish each meeting 15 – 30 minutes early.
- **Involve everyone** – as a meeting leader, ensure that you involve all participants and pursue opportunities to solicit input.
- **Participate** – as a participant, feel free to ask about the purpose of a meeting, the agenda, your role, etc. Be prepared to participate and be involved.
- **Eliminate** – limit attendance to only people who need to attend. Don't hesitate to speak up if you feel you or others don't need to be involved.
- **Question** – the need for any meeting held on a regular basis or agenda topics that are the same, meeting after meeting.
- **Document** – ensure someone is acting as a meeting recorder/scribe who will then issue follow-up action items, accountability assignments, timelines, etc., ideally within 48 hours after a meeting.
- **Go with the flow** – formal meetings that are well planned are important. So are informal meetings

that just happen. Know which type of meeting will best serve your purposes and achieve your results.

- **Silence is acceptance** – if you can't attend a meeting, provide input in advance. If you don't provide input, people will assume you're in agreement.
- **Support the outcome** – often the goal of 100% consensus is neither reasonable nor realistic. In such situations, strive for an 80% solution, 90% consensus, and 100% commitment. Remember, whether you're in agreement or not, it's important to publicly support the group efforts.

We strongly encourage you to review these guidelines and carefully consider how they can be applied to how you manage your involvement in meetings. Hopefully this will give you an opportunity to consider your meeting schedule and make some changes.

Summary

Organizations are always looking for quick methods to increase their profitability and effectiveness. In many, especially head office or service-type organizations, the HR costs constitute a major expense item. For organizations in which people spend a significant amount of time in meetings, it might be wise for management to pay some attention to how such a significant time-consuming item is being managed.

The history of ethics is a history of contradiction, not a history of progress.
– Michael Ignatieff, Author and Television Personality

Chapter 18

Ethical Behaviour in Business Organizations

In Chapter 2, we identified several reasons why organizations don't perform at their full potential. One reason we didn't mention was ethical behaviour. Although this may be less visible than some other issues undermining the performance of organizations, unethical behaviour has the potential to cause very severe damage to an organization, and such damage can last for a long time – and can even be deadly.

A few years ago, people might have paid passing attention to this topic. Every organization probably had some bad apples, but in general it wasn't considered to be a major problem. However, things have changed. The risk to a company's reputation is now very present in the minds of the boards of directors and senior executives. The electronic age and the advent of the Internet have made it much easier for people to spread news, and as a result have amplified the reputation risk manifold as compared to 20 or 25 years ago. Well-publicized cases have also raised the level of awareness. However, I'm not sure how much time people have invested reflecting on the topic. I hope this chapter will contribute to put some form of framework around it.

What has gone wrong?

We've witnessed an increase in the number of cases involving unethical behaviour, or at least it may be that known cases are more widely covered by the media. This may be due to a number of reasons. However, I think that an overaggressive approach to meeting artificial business goals has to rank quite high in explaining why we have seen an increased visibility. I also believe that people have become incrementally more *elastic* in what they consider to be acceptable and unacceptable. In addition to well-publicized cases in very large U.S. companies, we've also seen cases where people have stretched their comfort level as to what's ethical. Here are a few examples:

- Employees of financial institutions were trading for their own benefit, based on advanced information on unitized funds, resulting in lower returns for other unit holders. They couldn't figure out what they were doing wrong. They believed they weren't hurting anyone, even though they were enriching themselves in the process.
- Employees of investment firms and mutual fund companies were manipulating the closing values or allowing transactions that shouldn't be allowed, to increase volumes or embellish sales and investment performance.
- Professional firms were offering sports event tickets to clients and charging them back in a hidden way on regular bills.

I believe accidents can happen. Sometimes employees will do unpredictable things. However, in most cases senior executives should bear a major portion of the blame when unethical behaviour has taken place. In many cases, they have laid the foundation for disaster to happen and then they're surprised when it does.

What's the root cause of unethical behaviour?

- **Deficient hiring practices**. Sometimes employers hire people who are prone to unethical behaviour, either because of past history, or their reputation to get things done at any cost. Sometimes they're hired because they're *results focused* and don't let obstacles get in their way.

- **Unrealistic expectations placed on people**. Organizations try to do the best they can for stakeholders. However, in the process they may be expecting more than what's reasonable, and sometimes employees will find ways to deliver on these expectations, even if it means bending the rules.

- **Faulty incentive compensation programs**. Organizations that are very results focused have put aggressive incentive compensation programs in place, and in the absence of adequate controls, these may be an invitation for people to do whatever it takes to maximize payouts.

- **Expectation of quick turnaround**. A lot of pressure is placed on publicly-traded companies to show quick improvement in results. This may also be an invitation to lose sight of what's moral, legal and ethical.

- **Lack of proper controls**. Obviously, weak controls both in process and results will amplify any potential problems generated by unethical behaviour.
- **Culture of heroes**. At different times organizations elevate groups of people, a division, a subsidiary, or an individual to *hero* status for their achievements. However, this is also a signal to the rest of the organization that these people or organizations should be left alone to enjoy continued success. I believe a lot of unethical behaviour originates from this practice.
- **Greed**. This is an obvious cause. However, I'm not sure how prevalent it is. A lot of ethical issues have been with people who had no obvious need for additional money.
- **Laziness**. Sometimes people go for quick results and try to cut corners to get to the results more quickly.
- **Everybody-else-does-it mentality**. A lot of companies have found themselves in trouble over this because people came to believe there could be nothing wrong if others did the same.
- **Morality stretch**. I've been amazed at how comfortable people become at explaining the unexplainable. My experience is that in business and in politics, people can explain almost anything if they try hard enough!
- **Results-at-any-cost culture**. Some organizations keep communicating to their employees that targets need to be met regardless of circumstances. There's a fine line to walk between providing challenging targets and inviting people to *cheat* to meet them. If people believe that the end justifies the means, they'll take whatever means are required.

- **Excessive spending at senior levels**. There have been well-publicized cases of excessive spending by executives. These are very extreme cases. However, excessive spending also exists in more modest forms in some organizations, and when it does, it contributes to widen the ethical range among the rest of employees.
- **Good news culture**. In some organizations, executives like good news and don't want to hear bad news. So people create good news at any cost, give the good news, and nobody passes on the bad news or potential problems looming on the horizon.

Critical steps to minimize the risk of unethical behaviour

People are people, and it'll always be impossible to completely eliminate unethical behaviour. However, organizations can take a number of positive steps to minimize the risk by creating a culture that favours ethical behaviour. There's no magical recipe to this. It involves continuous action over extended periods of time on multiple fronts including:

- Creating a strong set of company values to be used by people as a reference point.
- Communicating and ongoing reinforcing of such values to all employees. It's also important to include new employees as they come on board.
- Senior people need to live these values and preach by example. Talking about ethics is important, but people take their cues from what they observe of the senior people.

- Senior people need to be close enough to their organization to extend their reach beyond their immediate staff. They must be able to develop a sense for what's happening in the organization by talking to people. Hopefully, employees will have enough trust to go to senior people if they feel something wrong is happening in the organization.
- There should be a culture of mutual trust, so people can trust executives to take the proper action if they're informed of wrongdoing within their organization. Sometimes people don't blow the whistle for fear of retribution or they believe issues will be ignored.
- Business plans should be built on a realistic basis with some amount of stretch. Overstretched plans are an invitation to ignore the targets or cut corners to get there. If plans are overly ambitious, senior executives need to apply the *smell test* and determine how these overstretched plans will be met.
- Spend some time communicating to people the difference between *legal* and *ethical*. Sometimes it may be legal but unethical. A very useful test is to question how stakeholders would react if they really understood how the organization is behaving. If the answer is *negatively*, there's a good chance it may be unethical.
- If a compliance function doesn't exist, consider creating one. If one already does, determine how to give it some teeth (some appropriate freedom of action to keep the organization out of trouble) without becoming an impediment to doing business.

- Stay away from the *herd* mentality. The test of ethical behaviour shouldn't be whether everybody else already does it. I certainly understand the pressure to keep up with the competition. However, this type of herd mentality has caused a lot of trouble in many organizations.
- Lastly, always remember that if it appears too good to be true, it probably is. Apply the smell test and ask questions until it makes sense to you – or until it doesn't.

Other observations

In addition to the several issues raised earlier, a couple of other issues deserve some attention. First, international diversification increases the risk of unethical behaviour. Different cultures have different definitions of what constitutes ethical behaviour, and increases the challenge of communicating acceptable ethical behaviour. Moreover, distance and multiple languages increase the difficulty in monitoring how people really conduct their business.

I'd also like to make special mention about sales organizations, especially those with heavy commission schedules. The more dependent people are on selling for immediate survival, the more present may be the temptation to widen the range of acceptability in behaviour. This is not to say the majority of salespeople are unethical. It simply tends to be a higher risk area and as with any risk, needs to be assessed and monitored.

Summary

There's currently a high level of awareness of the need for ethical behaviour. However, I think there's still a gap between what executives say they want to see happening, and what they're prepared to do to make it happen. It costs time and money to put in place an environment which will maximize the chance the organization will behave ethically as an entity. It's also a distraction from the rest of the more visible revenue-generating activities. However, the alternatives are few. Organizations either do what they have to do or face the perspective of doing a postmortem at some point wondering, *Why did it happen to us?*

I was underpaid for the first half of my life;
I don't mind being overpaid for the second half.
  – Pierre Berton, Author

Chapter 19

Incentive Compensation Program (ICP) – Motivator, Cash Cow or Nuisance?

There are a couple of reasons why I waited so long to comment on ICP. First, I believe ICP is a tool that can pull together everything else that has already been put into place, to create the right organization with the right people, the right processes, and the proper management structure (including good leaders and managers). However, there's also another more profound reason why I've handled a number of other topics before getting to this one. Essentially, this is where it belongs as far as truly motivating people – quite low in the pecking order.

As an employee, I liked ICP. In fact, I liked it a lot, especially at payout time. The more it paid out, the more I liked it! As an executive having to administer ICP, I didn't like it quite as much. I had my doubts as to how much of a motivator it really was, and I was painfully aware of how much time we needed to invest in administering it.

Chapter 19—Incentive Compensation Program (ICP) – Motivator, Cash Cow or Nuisance?

138

Let's examine some observations on ICP from a user perspective. It's not meant to be totally balanced but rather to highlight some of the flaws I've observed over the years. I'm also very conscious that this book is likely to be read by several people working in consulting firms that specialize in developing ICP, including a couple of very capable compensation consultants. So, once again, I'm not an expert, just a fairly sophisticated ICP user.

Why do we have incentive compensation?

- To be competitive with the rest of the marketplace. Essentially, most private and some public sector organizations offer ICP as part of the total compensation package. It would be very difficult to attract valuable candidates without an ICP in place.
- If the ICP is well structured, it may be a major tool to focus the organization toward the elements that matter to it.
- ICP is really a variable form of compensation, which means it's not guaranteed. Employees may look at this as additional compensation. From a company perspective, ICP is budgeted at some predetermined level assuming that results are going to be on target. If results are above target, there's more ICP being paid out but everybody is happy. If results are below target, especially earnings, ICP pays less than budgeted and the earnings underperformance is mitigated by budgeted ICP being released into earnings.

Why doesn't incentive compensation always meet its objectives?

- In general, there's a fair amount of time required to administer ICP properly (setting and evaluating objectives, systems work, calculations, pay and communications). The time invested must be subtracted from any productivity gained because of ICP.

- ICP creates as many behavioural problems as it solves. I've seen ICP create silos. These silos may be at the national, regional, divisional, or departmental level, or between subsidiaries. No matter what's measured, time needs to be invested to make sure people don't create silos. On the other hand, if what's measured is too broad (total company) then ICP may lose its impact.

- ICP is supposed to keep people focused; however, sometimes people become focused on the wrong things. As an example, I'm convinced that overly aggressive ICPs are the cause of some unethical behaviour. For example, a manager not allowing people to go on training programs to come under budget, when budget is one of the elements being measured as part of ICP.

- ICP can impede teamwork. If measurements are based mostly on individual performance, ratings are seen as subjective, and may encourage people to focus on their own performance, or perception of it, at the expense of team performance. If everything is team based or company based, it leaves limited room for great individual performers to be rewarded, and the good performers complain they're not being rewarded appropriately.

Chapter 19—Incentive Compensation Program (ICP) — Motivator, Cash Cow or Nuisance?

140

- ICP may encourage people to focus on the short-term. Sometimes there are long-term ICPs put in place to keep things in balance. My experience has always been that short-term will win over long-term.
- For people at higher levels, ICP tends to include a fairly significant earnings component as this is of great interest to stockholders and other stakeholders. There are a couple of issues associated with this. In some industries, earnings can be managed to some extent through so-called one-time adjustments, and therefore earnings may not be truly reflective of efforts and impact. Another issue is that when ICP is earnings based, it almost becomes a proxy for a profit-sharing plan. This may generate adequate payouts but may not achieve what was intended.
- ICP tends to work best when things are going well (when everybody makes money and everybody is happy). On the other hand, it doesn't work quite as well when results are poor or when things are difficult. The best employees (those who are the most in demand and most likely to be offered attractive jobs elsewhere) will have limited incentives to stay under bad conditions, unless some other special arrangements are put in place.

What can be done to improve how incentive compensation works?

As we all realize, there's no perfect answer to the challenges created by the presence of ICP. It's well understood that not having ICP is generally not an option in a competitive environment. However, there are a few things that can be done to improve ICP:

- If ICP produces results similar to a profit-sharing plan in a given organization, it might be simpler to have a profit-sharing plan. It might be easier to administer, may reduce design work, and facilitate employee communication. [If we (the company) make money, you make money. If we don't, you don't!]
- Simplicity has to be an important design element of any ICP. There's only so much focus that can be controlled through ICP. It's not possible to optimize it on every possible element. Organizations need to decide what really matters and focus measurements on these very few elements.
- Complex calculations to evaluate payout amounts should be discouraged. I've seen actuaries use very complex formulas to calculate individual ICP payout. I could hardly understand what was done. (Off the record, I'm an actuary myself; so believe me, the formulas were bad.)
- Finally, organizations try to direct behaviours through ICP. However, there's likely to be much higher leverage through adequate leadership to inspire and motivate people. If the main source of people motivation were a generous ICP, I think this is a sign of trouble. When people are passionate about something, such as politics, community activities, fundraising, etc., they don't need ICP to motivate them because they're passionate about the causes they espouse. I understand ICP as a source of competitive compensation; I'm much more lukewarm with the idea that this is required to motivate people.

Chapter 19—Incentive Compensation Program (ICP) – Motivator, Cash Cow or Nuisance?

142

Other observations

Based on prior experience:

- The best performers I've had the opportunity to have under my leadership weren't primarily motivated by ICP. They expected to be paid competitively; however, ICP didn't drive them any harder. I made it my business to make sure they were well rewarded, and they focused on their work.
- I've had mostly negative experiences with people who were primarily motivated by ICP. In general, they didn't turn out to be great performers. ICP payout isn't a substitute for passion and commitment.
- ICP can be pretty challenging as far as balancing individual and team objectives. As a tool to promote team behaviour, it has its limits. My experience is that people who are team focused will do what's right for the team, sometimes at the expense of immediate personal financial rewards. When people need ICP to motivate them to be team players, they may not be the people you want around your organization.
- ICP may be quite helpful to influence behaviour when people have full control over their environment. Some sales jobs may be perfect for ICP or direct commissions. In consulting environments, ICP based on billable work might be a win-win situation, assuming there's unlimited work, which is seldom the case. Then, if billable hours represent a key component, there's always an issue when people are asked to work on some infrastructure projects.

In general, most programs need flexibility and judgement to accommodate changing circumstances.

- In sales environments, especially complex corporate sales, targets should be team based. I've worked in an organization where sales were individual based. Every sale needed to be split between numbers of individuals. Then people would go on sales calls alone, if they could, to avoid having to split the sales credits. What a mess!
- As a last thought, I would be curious to see ICP's real impact on productivity. I realize this isn't easy to measure. Ideally, it's best to measure two different environments assuming everything else is equal, and this is seldom the case. I'm sure the introduction of ICP and changes in ICP design may have an immediate impact; however, I'm not so sure about its lasting impact, once people have been accustomed to some kind of payout fluctuating around some average.

Summary

Despite my earlier comments, I'm sure ICP is here to stay. I'm not suggesting it should disappear. However, I think that employers have to be very conscious of the limitations and potential negative impact if not designed and implemented carefully. Also, I believe there needs to be awareness that ICP isn't an adequate substitution for motivation and commitment generated through good leadership and management techniques. ICP may be a good support tool but it's just a support element, not a driver of organizational behaviour.

The most rewarding part of management is working with people.
The worst part of management is working with people.
  – George Torok, Motivational Speaker

Chapter 20

Human Resources (HR) – Strategic Leader or Poor Cousin?

Initially, the various chapters of this book were published in the form of monthly newsletters. After a few of these newsletters had been distributed, one of the recipients sent me a note asking whether I would cover a specific topic that was of concern to her:

> *I wonder if in your upcoming issues you could address your views on what HR's role should be in an organization. I find that at times they communicate very poorly, and lose sight of business issues to comply with poorly devised policies, which aren't communicated nor applied consistently. I was wondering, having worked in a big organization, if you had similar issues, and how these issues were handled.*

Well, it just so happens the view expressed here is far from unique. In fact, this is fairly common in many organizations. Like many people, I complained about HR, and then I became a country head with an HR area of 70 people or so reporting to me. This is when I went from complaining and making suggestions to

Chapter 20—Human Resources (HR) – Strategic Leader or Poor Cousin?

146

finally having an opportunity to put my thinking into practice. I found this to be a fascinating and rewarding experience.

What's the exact role of HR?

My experience is that in many organizations the role of HR isn't very well defined. When I started in the business 30 years ago, the department was referred to as *Personnel Administration*, and over the years has evolved into a *Human Resources Management* area. The major issue is that the thinking has not always evolved at the same pace as the terminology. Many people in HR see themselves in personnel administration. A lot of their internal clients also see them that way, and worst of all, many executives including CEOs see and treat them as such. So it's no surprise there's some amount of frustration among HR employees, and among their internal clients.

A key issue that leads to confusion is that in most organizations, HR is expected to play several roles. Among others, they have to deal with:

- strategic position of the firm in the area of HR
- policy setting
- compensation and benefits practices
- policing the practices that have been established
- transaction execution
- supporting role in hiring and firing people
- delivery of other services such as training, etc.

Some of these roles are conflicting at times. So a critical element is to prioritize where the emphasis is going to be. Is this going to be a strategic unit or a support unit focused on operations? Typically, the answer has to come from the CEO or whoever has responsibility for a major division where HR reports. Then, it's important that it's clear in everyone's mind where HR is going to focus – will they focus on the transactional aspect or on the more strategic issues, while paying appropriate attention to the more routine aspects of their jobs?

One of the major reasons why HR has attracted a fair amount of negative criticism in many organizations is because of the policing role they have been assigned or have decided to play. In most organizations, there's major resentment toward HR because of this. In some, this is the result of a lack of cohesiveness as operational managers have been allowed to *dump* their unpleasant HR-related duties on HR, and are quick to blame HR for everything they don't like to do. It's critical that operational managers assume their responsibility with respect to policing HR-related activities.

I see HR's responsibility as the enhancement of HR capabilities within the organization. This includes getting the right people, coordinating training, enhancing leadership capabilities, coordinating appropriate remedial action for nonperformers, ensuring that compensation practices allow the organization to have access to the right people, and finally, executing or coordinating the processing of transactions required for policies to be applied within the organization.

Chapter 20—Human Resources (HR) – Strategic Leader or Poor Cousin?

148

What does HR need to discharge its responsibilities?

A key element required to allow HR to play its role effectively is a clear message from the CEO (or equivalent depending on the size of the organization) to the rest of the organization as to the nature of the mandate it has been given. Then the CEO needs to support HR in his/her communications and *actions*. The CEO's behaviour will have a major impact on how HR is treated within the organization.

Then, HR needs to be treated as an equal partner to the business units as opposed to being treated as the poor cousin. It goes without saying that HR needs to earn the respect of business units, and earn the right to be treated as an equal partner around the management table. In many organizations, HR is treated as a cost centre, not a revenue-generating centre, and the end result is it tends to be at the bottom of the pile in terms of priorities. I suggest that HR must be looked at and treated as a revenue-generating centre, even though the revenue side is difficult to measure. If your human capital isn't revenue producing, I wonder what else revenue generation is? The fact that revenue is difficult to measure and that HR doesn't always play its role the way it should is beside the point. If HR is broken, it has to be fixed – but it has to be allowed to contribute to revenue generation through enhancing human capital.

Last but not least, HR has to be positioned properly within the organization as it sets the tone as to how the president or the CEO perceives HR. There may be practical issues to consider; however, HR should report to the top. Initially, I made the mistake of having it report to somebody else but I quickly corrected this as I concluded if I were to influence people capabilities, HR had to be actively involved and I needed to interact with them all the time. Many organizations have some HR people attached to the business units to deal with day-to-day applications of HR policies. I've generally found this model to produce very good results, as long as you have the right HR people assigned to these business units.

People and tools

Over the years, I've always been amazed by the lack of human touch exhibited by many people in HR. You'd think you need to have great skills in human interaction to be effective in an HR role; however, this doesn't appear to be the case all the time. One of the reasons is that there has been so much emphasis on the so-called *HR professional* label that has been used over the last few years. So, in some organizations, HR ends up with HR people who are professionally knowledgeable in training, compensation, benefits, labour negotiations and employment practices, but many aren't trained or don't possess the skills to deal effectively with people.

My view has always been that for most employees, when they refer to *the company*, they refer to what they observe from their first-line manager and HR. So if the HR area is going to be the face of the organization, they should represent the values you want to put in place within the organization. A few years ago, we had an employee survey that showed the most negative responses came from our HR area. This became a grave source of concern

Chapter 20—Human Resources (HR) – Strategic Leader or Poor Cousin?

150

as it was difficult to imagine that people who felt so negative about their work would project a positive image to current and future employees, and we made appropriate changes to make sure this wouldn't be repeated going forward.

In addition to technical skills required to operate in HR, these characteristics are also necessary:

- Interpersonal skills.
- Communication abilities.
- Project management skills to ensure projects get executed on time and on budget.
- Process minded, so that work gets executed in an orderly fashion.
- Business minded – this is lacking in many HR people which makes it difficult for many to be taken seriously by business units.
- High energy and contagious enthusiasm for the organization, as this is what they must *sell* to the rest of the organization and to potential employees.

Last but not least, HR people need to be lead by people who are business minded. Either a trained HR person with a good business mind, or a business person with a strong HR inclination can do a good job. Alternating between an HR-trained person and a general manager coming from the business side may work well to bring different skills at various times.

On the tools aspect, HR needs appropriate tools, especially on the technology side. For a variety of reasons, organizations tend to cut back on HR projects because the impact is obvious right away on the expense side – but it may take quite some time to show up on the revenue side. Sometimes the inability of some HR managers to prioritize properly may be why their demands aren't always taken seriously. Finally, several organizations have gone toward outsourcing to avoid having to deal directly with the more mundane aspects of HR (the transactional side). The future will tell whether this brings about the expected benefits.

Accountability

In several organizations, HR-specific accountabilities are ill defined. The end result is that HR is measured in terms of action as opposed to results. They get measured in terms of initiating and completing projects, and processing transactions, as opposed to being measured in terms of their real impact on the organization. Critical impact factors will vary from organization to organization; however, what matters is that they have specific and relevant accountabilities, the same as business units. Leadership effectiveness, employee surveys, absenteeism, budgets, turnover, etc., are all factors to be taken into account when measuring HR, as well as feedback from business units as far as measuring their value added to the organization.

Summary

For any organization, results are driven by people. Whether it's technology, marketing, finance, client service or sales, everything originates from the ability of people to develop and execute business models. In this context, it's amazing that many

Chapter 20—Human Resources (HR) – Strategic Leader or Poor Cousin?

152

organizations underinvest in the leading source of success for the future. A great place to start is to ensure there's a properly staffed and organized HR area that can act as the key enabler for this important aspect of the business. For organizations that have neglected this component, it's a potentially high-return investment.

You have to know what you don't know when you play the stock market.
    – Alexander Tadich, Stock Trader and Writer

Chapter 21

Tell Me, Which Shareholder Are We Talking About?

Over the course of my career, I've had the opportunity to work directly or indirectly with organizations operating under different ownership structures. I've been associated with government-operated agencies, mutual companies, privately-held corporations, partnerships, and finally publicly-traded companies. I was also very involved in the process of implementing the transformation of a mutual company into a stock company.

To me, stock companies have always represented the ultimate form of ownership. They represent the purest form of capitalism with easier and potentially unlimited access to capital, open disclosure, potential for lining up the interests of management and shareholders, and ultimate accountability to shareholders.

Unfortunately, many publicly-traded companies fail to realize their full potential due to a lack of clarity in identifying which shareholders they're trying to serve. Is management attempting to serve the best interests of the shareholder who bought five years ago and will likely hold the stock for several years to come? Is it trying to serve the interests of the shareholder who bought yesterday and may sell tomorrow if the price is right? Or, is it trying to represent some shareholder in-between these two groups?

If asked the question, many executives might answer that they try to serve the best interests of all these groups. To me, this is a *non-answer* as it's nearly impossible to serve the interests of all these shareholders at the same time, especially the shareholders at the extremes (those who buy and hold and the frequent traders).

Although this last chapter isn't directly connected with the rest of this book, I felt it was worthwhile to include. For a publicly-traded company, the view taken by management on shareholder issues is likely to greatly influence how the organization is being managed. If management adopts a very short-term focus as a result of shareholder expectations, the organization is highly unlikely to be built on a sustainable basis for the future.

What's the issue?

Essentially this would be a non-issue if management were able to serve equally well all groups of shareholders. If this were the case, there would be no need to specify which group of shareholders would take priority. However, I don't believe it's possible to serve all groups of shareholders equally well. In the absence of specific choices being made, most executive groups will feel pressured to satisfy the short-term demands of shareholders (those shareholders with a shorter time horizon, the more frequent traders). In this process, I believe that loyal long-term horizon investors are likely to be shortchanged in their expectations. They believe they're buying the stock of a company with a long-term horizon while they may be investing in a company that has a short-term horizon, with varying degrees of consideration given to the long-term.

What's the underlying cause?

Simply stated, the cause of all this is quite human. The pressure on management to deliver short-term results is enormous. It's easier for management to attempt to deliver short-term results based on somewhat unrealistic expectations than it is to explain a complex long-term game plan that may involve peaks and valleys.

There are several reasons why management is under so much pressure to deliver short-term results:

- Many financial analysts tend to be very focused on quarterly results. Management doesn't look forward to explaining underperformance on the quarterly analyst calls. Among the analysts, many of them represent firms whose general focus is on customers who trade as opposed to those who buy and hold. The retail securities market, mutual funds, hedge funds, and the short-term performance focus in the pension investment area, are all elements contributing to the focus on short-term results. There's nothing wrong with the way analysts do their job;

it's only that their role and the customers they represent need to be kept in mind by company management.

- The market has come to expect management to *smooth out* what's happening in the economy. As an example, in the financial sector, results should be expected to fluctuate depending on the economy, but more importantly, depending on what's happening in the financial markets. Yet there's some expectation that management will continue to produce steadily increasing results, despite the fact that informed shareholders would expect some fluctuation in those results.

- The media put a lot of pressure on producing steady results, meaning again that management must try to minimize natural fluctuations. The media tend to jump on the opportunity to portray management in a bad light whenever it *fails* to produce expected results, so the temptation is to smooth out results. A difficult issue for management is the fact that the public in general may confuse stock performance with the financial stability of the organization, which may lead to a negative impact on the company brand and sales.

- The board of directors will also put pressure on management to perform. This is their role. There's nothing wrong with the board putting some heat on management as long as it understands what it's asking for and what it's really getting. Good short-term results don't always lead to good long-term results. A strong board is able to balance the two.

- The average tenure of CEOs has been shortening for a variety of reasons. No point taking a 20-year horizon if the average stay is going to be around 5 years or sometimes shorter, based on figures quoted by the media.

- Finally, management is remunerated both on short-term and long-term performance, which seems to be fine until we look a little more closely. On the short-term side, annual bonuses tend to be determined on 12-month performance with the financial component typically being most important. Lack of performance will affect everyone on a bonus scheme, including middle management. Low bonuses become a morale, retention and recruiting issue. On the long-term side, options have been the favoured instrument for rewarding management. However, options aren't quite a perfect match as far as aligning the interests of management with those of long-term horizon shareholders. This topic has been well documented lately. As a result, several boards have been taking a proactive approach as far as modifying long-term incentive plans. Restricted, performance, and deferred share units are all likely to be part of the new arrangements, and are likely to be accompanied by performance measures and restrictions on the ability of executives to exercise these incentives.

Impact on company operations

In general, operations have a difficult time adapting to a management style that focuses on short-term results. In some industries, due to the cyclical nature of the business, operations are structured in a way such that they react quickly to a changing economy. However, there are several companies operating through very long cycles. Again, using the financial sector as an example, typically companies have very long-term relationships with clients; they transact loans that are repayable over long periods, make long-term investments, and may sell products creating liabilities to be met several decades later.

Generally, short-term focus on results is reflected through one or several actions:

- Staff reduction or hiring freeze even though this may be at the expense of client service.
- Freeze on training programs even though it may be at the expense of longer-term productivity.
- Postponement of technology investments even though these may be justified for the long-term success of the enterprise.

The long-term impact of these measures is real but might not be reflected in the company's performance for quite some time. However, you can expect one or more of these outcomes:

- Confusion among employees who can't understand whether management has a plan and whether they believe in it and stick to it.
- Disappointment among clients who may fail to see the long-term commitment of their supplier toward their business.
- Short-term savings tend to have a ripple effect. The idea is that these budget cuts should be temporary and will be made up in the following period. However, this tends not to happen. For example, let's assume that an organization

has an information technology (IT) budget of $10M and decides to reduce it by 10% for the current year to $9M. The following year, going back to the same level as that budgeted for the current year will result in an increase of $1M or 11.1%. If the organization wishes to catch up on the work postponed, then it's looking at $11M spending as compared to $9M or a 22.2% increase. Most organizations will balk at this type of increase, even though it may have been just to get back on the original plan.

- Operational divisions have difficulty planning, as budget cuts may not be related to the financial health of specific divisions or units.
- Support divisions such as HR become an easy target for quick savings, and typically never get to deliver on their promises or meet expectations from operating divisions, and quickly acquire a reputation for being unreliable partners.

So, what's the solution?

This is a tough question. It's much easier to criticize the situation than to be creative and come up with solutions. Here are a few ideas:

- Companies spend a lot of time producing mission and vision statements that sometimes turn out to be meaningless to a good portion of their employees, either because they don't understand what is meant, or because management acts in a way that doesn't support the statements. Time should be invested to increase clarity on the nature of the shareholders who'll best be served by investing in the company. A commitment to take action for the sole benefit of long-term shareholders, for example, would help focus on meeting this objective, and would provide real substance to the mission and vision statements.

- Better alignment of bonuses and long-term incentives with the interests of shareholders who have been identified as the target shareholder group.
- To the extent possible, better communication with the financial market with respect to the shareholder group being best served by an investment in the company, and reinforcement of actions being taken to be true to the commitment, even though it might mean more volatility in short-term results. Some companies have followed this approach in the past with some success.

A Final Word

I started writing this book in the form of monthly newsletters to help market my services. However, I also felt there was a gap in knowledge and application when it came to organizational leadership and management. Nearly two years have elapsed since I started writing these articles. During this time, I've had several opportunities to work with different organizations on a consulting basis. As I'm about to return to near full-time, hands-on management, I feel it's appropriate to reflect on what I've observed over these last two years.

Based on my recent experience both with clients and other organizations, I must conclude that there's still a huge gap between the competencies required to run organizations, and the level of proficiency exhibited by many executives and senior managers. I feel that people are still ill-prepared to step into management and senior leadership roles. In several instances, the art of leadership and management is still often practised at a very basic level. New managers are often not well prepared for the challenges facing them. They lack a complete framework to discharge their responsibilities at a high level of proficiency.

In many organizations, there's too much emphasis on short-term results. People are anxious to make their mark and produce quick results. However, running an organization is like running a marathon. If marathon runners don't perform basic training properly, they're unlikely to be successful in completing a marathon. Likewise, organizations that don't have the patience needed to establish a solid base are unlikely to enjoy success in the long run.

I don't have any illusions about this book being a recipe for success for everybody in every circumstance. This was never the intent. I wanted to offer one form of comprehensive framework to run an organization. I also wanted to share some ideas which hopefully would help some people become better managers and better leaders. Foremost, I hoped this would be a good tool to allow people to spend a bit of time reflecting on how they want to lead their organization.

An organization is like a machine. It has some potential output which is often unrealized because of major leaks. If this book helps some of you identify sources of leakage and to correct them, then I'll feel the writing was well worth the effort.

References

Chapter

1	Reference 1 (See bottom of page)
2	Reference 1
3	Website: www.bartleby.com
4	Reference 2
5	Reference 1
6	Website: www.quotationspage.com
7	Reference 2
8	Reference 2
9	Reference 2
10	Reference 1
11	Reference 1
12	Reference 2
13	Website: www.quotationspage.com
14	Reference 2
15	Website: www.quotationspage.com
16	Reference 2
17	Reference 2
18	Reference 1
19	Reference 2
20	Reference 2
21	Reference 2

Reference 1
Colombo, John Robert. *The Dictionary of Canadian Quotations*. Toronto: Stoddart, 1991.

Reference 2
Colombo, John Robert. *Famous Lasting Words – Great Canadian Quotations*. Vancouver: Douglas & McIntyre, 2000.